Police Reform in the United States

Vollmer in the early 1950s, working in his Berkeley home. He was active as a police consultant and writer during the years following his retirement from teaching and police work. Courtesy Bancroft Library.

Police Reform in the United States

the United States

The Era of August Vollmer, 1905-1932

by Gene E. Carte
and Elaine H. Carte

UNIVERSITY OF CALIFORNIA PRESS
Berkeley · Los Angeles · London

363.2
Car

University of California Press
Berkeley and Los Angeles, California

University of California Press, Ltd.
London, England

Copyright © 1975, by
The Regents of the University of California

ISBN: 0-520-02599-7
Library of Congress Catalog Card Number: 73-87248
Printed in the United States of America

To Jane and Gary Robinson

Contents

Preface

In the short run, it often appears that the institution of policing attracts an endless amount of tinkering and interference; strident suggestions for reform or retrenchment come from groups who are dissatisfied with police policies, or who believe that procedural restrictions limit the policeman in his job.

However, there have been few basic changes in the structure of American policing since the nineteenth century when it was first established in the nation's growing urban centers. The most important reorientation during the current century has been the acceptance of professionalism as an occupational model. Most changes that are taking place today are essentially consistent with the goals and techniques of the professional model.

Because one of the dominant characteristics of professionalism is the facade of expertise or "knowing better," many citizens feel intimidated in their attempts to monitor the workings of criminal justice agencies—including the police—in their communities. This book is intended to offer readers a critical and historical perspective from which they can evaluate those aspects of American policing that derive from the professional model. We also hope that this perspective will assist students of criminal justice in understanding the origins of some of the important premises of the field.

We have focused here upon the social and occupational factors that were instrumental in bringing about the acceptance of police professionalism. There has been no attempt to be comprehensive in presenting the technical advances that accompanied the development of professionalism. Instead, we hope to cast light upon the present adequacy of the professional model by exploring the ideas that nurtured its roots.

The basic research for this work was done at the School of Criminology at the University of California in Berkeley. This school was established in 1950 because of the influence of August Vollmer, who, as chief of police in Berkeley for many years, believed strongly in the need for educated policemen and for research into criminological problems. It was perhaps natural that an increasing interest in police professionalism led to our study of Vollmer's career as the foremost advocate of that model. At the same time, we worked with others to develop an oral history of Vollmer's work and influence upon others.

The present volume draws upon material from Gene Carte's dissertation on Vollmer and police professionalism and from further records of that time that have recently been acquired by the Bancroft Library. Elaine Carte has been involved in this research and has performed most of the job of revising the dissertation and incorporating the new materials for this book.

For their constructive criticisms and encouragement during various stages of this work we should like to thank Professors Jerome Skolnick, Eugene Lee, Paul Takagi, and Sheldon Messinger. We should also like to thank John D. Holstrom, former chief of police in Berkeley. We are grateful for the assistance of the staff of the Bancroft Library, especially Willa Baum of the Regional Oral History Office and Estelle Rebec of the Manuscripts Division.

In addition, we should like to acknowledge the financial assistance of the National Institute of Law Enforcement and Criminal Justice during the earlier years of this research.

Gene E. Carte
Elaine H. Carte
July 1974

Introduction

When policing began to be called a "profession" or "science" back in the early years of this century, it was the start of an attempt to bring functional order and dignity into a disorganized, low-status occupation. At this time, graft, incompetence, and brutality were common within big city police departments, which were manned by officers who were haphazardly selected, poorly trained, and underpaid. Policemen were under constant political pressure to enforce the laws according to the interests of those in power but were at the same time being attacked by vocal reformers for the vice and crime that seemed to many city dwellers to be rising without control.

To reformers of August Vollmer's generation, the greatest evil confronting public service was political corruption in the cities. Their concern with the tendency of political officials to compromise and contaminate the workings of public service agencies was almost obsessive in character. Leonhard Fuld summed up the pervasive nature of the problem when he wrote in 1909, "Corruption and dishonesty are found everywhere in public life and are not entirely unknown in private life. The citizens get as good a police service as they want."[1]

Thoughtful citizens and police leaders of the time hoped to rescue policemen from the perils of corruption and incompetence by turning

---

[1] *Police Administration: A Critical Study of Police Organisations in the United States and Abroad* (Montclair, N.J.: Patterson Smith, 1971, reprinted from 1909 ed.), p. 40.

1

their attention to policing *as an organization*. By 1920, several important books had been published by reform-minded scholars who described conditions in municipal police departments and recommended improvements. Unfavorable comparisons of American policing with European models formed the central theme of these studies.

Fuld's perceptive analysis of American policing was the first serious look at police administration and its relation to American political processes. Raymond Fosdick went abroad in 1913 to research an extensive study of the European police and concluded that it was "an excellent piece of machinery." He ascribed this excellence to the absence of unenforceable laws, to strong and independent leadership, and to superior selection and training of officers.[2] In 1920 he published a book analyzing American policing, which he excoriated as "a *job*, held, perhaps by the grace of some mysterious political influence, and conducted in an atmosphere sordid and unhealthy."[3]

Within policing, the dominant spokesman for police reform in this century was August Vollmer, who began his career in 1905 as the elected town marshal of Berkeley, California. While developing the Berkeley department, of which he was chief until 1932, Vollmer became the principal author of the professional model of policing. This model centered upon the concept of an idealized policeman who was a skilled and dedicated crime fighter, rigorously trained to perform a difficult job; who was aggressive in using science and technology in all phases of policing; and who was deeply involved in the community he served.

The best realization of this ideal within a working department was the Berkeley Police Department during the Vollmer years. Despite occasional absences to other cities, Vollmer retained a tight and intimate control over the small department he had developed. He sought out innovations and cultivated a power base in the town that supported his efforts to reform policing. He was also an able publicist who knew how to draw attention to accomplishments in Berkeley that other departments may have used with less vigor or success.

Vollmer's greatest influence, however, came through the substantial number of police administrators and educators who were trained in the Berkeley department or who studied with him in university

[2] *European Police Systems* (New York: The Century Co., 1915), pp. 384-385.
[3] *American Police Systems* (Montclair, N.J.: Patterson Smith, 1969, reprinted from 1920 ed.), pp. 379-380.

programs. O. W. Wilson was the most prominent of these. He developed a style of policing that derived from Vollmer, yet became distinctly different over the years when he was chief in Wichita and superintendent of the Chicago department. The Wilson model emphasized the efficient use of technical skills and equipment to suppress criminal acts and became more detached from the community than Vollmer's Berkeley model.

Professional policing arose in response to a combination of specific concerns felt by middle-class citizens, business leaders, and policemen during the early decades of this century. Urban pressures, distrust of immigrant groups, an exaggerated fear of crime, and the advent of widespread automobile use were significant realities of the day. The professional model answered many of the discontents on both sides: Policemen were able to lobby for the upgrading of internal standards, for higher pay, and for a larger share of community respect; and middle-class citizens and business leaders saw professional policing as an antidote to the corrupting influences of politics. The common denominator of a wide array of reform movements during those years was a profound distrust of the traditional American political processes, particularly in the cities.

It is the purpose of this study to trace the development of professional policing as an idea, principally through the career of August Vollmer, and to analyze its effect in restricting alternate models. Although few contemporary police departments may be said to meet the standards of professionalism for which Vollmer proselytized, the general acceptance of the model, with its corollaries of detachment, professional expertise, and definition of police function, has severely limited efforts by communities to alter or redefine the kind of policing they receive.

August Vollmer is the focus of this study because he did more than any other individual to originate and promote professional policing. Through his writings and teaching and by the example of his own department—probably the most effective and creative ever developed—Vollmer made the best case possible for the "new policing."

In these pages, use of the term "professionalism" is unavoidable because it is the accepted term to denote that model of policing which stands apart from politics and strives for objective and aggressive law enforcement. The difficulties of applying the concept of professionalism in its larger sense to American policing are discussed in Chapter 7.

When contemporary police leaders speak of professional policing, they are generally describing departments that are able to operate without undue political interference, that maintain modern training programs, and that use up-to-date techniques like computerized records systems and sophisticated communications. Most big city police departments direct their own expenditures of funds, efforts, and research based on the professional model, even though there is considerable local variation in the way the model is interpreted. Underlying the vagueness of the modern concept of professionalism is the larger ambiguity of American policing itself, an ambiguity which persists despite the efforts of Vollmer and others to bring unity and coherence to the police function.

1 THE CALL FOR REFORM

> One turns from the history of our municipal development
> with the wish that most of its sordid story could be blotted
> out.
>
> Fosdick, *American Police Systems*
> (1920), p. 117

A Problem of Function

Very little of the policeman's job actually involves crime fighting.
Only about two out of every ten police calls are related to crime;
the other eight are calls for other types of assistance. Even the
staunchest advocates of professionalism have recognized that policing
is predominantly a miscellaneous function.[1]

But crime fighting has come to be regarded as the most *important*
function of the police, despite the fact that many serious crimes—
homicide, rape, assault—are relatively inaccessible to police intervention. Vollmer and other police reformers believed that, in the interest
of police effectiveness in fighting crime, the police department should
be organized around this single function. Other tasks were seen as
necessary but secondary responsibilities.

A policeman today is monitored by his superiors in terms of
the arrest or citation activities he performs, and little incentive is
provided for performing other types of work. For example, both
Washington, D.C., and St. Louis attempted to set up detoxification
centers that would require active participation by patrolmen on the
beat. These efforts were sabotaged by the officers because they felt

---

[1] See James F. Ahern, *Police in Trouble* (New York: Hawthorn Books,
1972), pp. 168-169; and John Webster, *Police Task and Time Study* (Doctoral
dissertation, University of California, Berkeley, 1968).

they disturbed internal reward systems within the department that were based on "good" arrests.[2]

Even in performing their crime-fighting function, the police face the contradiction that the types of crime that are easiest to detect are those which are the most likely to be shielded by the community. Regularized or organized criminal activity depends upon the existence of a market for its services—gambling, prostitution, alcohol, and drugs—within the community. If this market exists, there is little help to be found in attempts to suppress the criminal activity.

Crime that is more individual or disorganized, on the other hand, will adapt its shape to meet whatever requirements the organizational structure of the police imposes upon it. The best defense against a good organization, in this case, is no organization at all, which may well characterize the structure of so much juvenile crime today. The "hit-or-miss" criminal activities of small groups of juveniles in cities like New York are an example of the type of crime with which a crime fighting police department is ill equipped to deal.[3]

Implicit in the crime-fighting stance of the police is also the problem of defining which crimes the police will fight. When "important" crime is defined as the types of crimes committed by poor and minority groups, very little policing is directed against middle-class crime. A centralized, crime-fighting police unit within a minority community focuses upon crimes committed by, not against, the local inhabitants. More sophisticated crimes like housing violations and merchant fraud are ignored or referred to the city bureaucracy. This is an inevitable consequence of organizing the police around a centrally defined mission.

In fact, there is no single function around which police operations may rationally be organized. Postal employees, firemen, or sanitation workers have jobs with one overriding purpose, despite whatever secondary activities may be attached to it. The policeman's job, on the other hand, lacks coherent function; it is the most poorly defined of the government services that organize and regulate life within a city. The policeman performs an assortment of tasks that become increasingly difficult to classify or to use as the basis for a national police philosophy.

[2] Raymond T. Nimmer, *Two Million Unnecessary Arrests* (Chicago: American Bar Foundation, 1970), pp. 116-118.
[3] For an excellent description of this kind of disorganized juvenile crime,

Bruce Smith wrote that the police are popularly known as those responsible for "suppressing crimes and public disorders, and regulating the use of the highways," although in the past they had worked in sanitation control or suppression of political activity. Policing "has even been expanded to cover practically all forms of public regulation and domestic order."[4]

In other words, policing has traditionally been a *miscellaneous government service* that is charged with responsibility for all the duties that do not fall within the purview of other established public agencies, and it is often the primary contact that a citizen has with his city government. The most miscellaneous of these duties are ones that have only a remote connection to the general welfare of the city. James Q. Wilson described the "service" functions of the police— "first aid, rescuing cats, helping ladies, and the like"—as being intended to "please the client and no one else." He noted that there was no reason in principle why they could not be performed by the private sector—"Emergency Services, Inc."[5]

By the last quarter of the nineteenth century, American municipal policing was losing some of the duties, like fire fighting and sanitation, that it had performed in earlier years. Police organization was in flux, in response to changing public expectations of what the police should do.

For example, in the 1870s a controversy arose among New Yorkers about the maintenance of the streets, which were traditionally cleaned by private companies who received contracts from the city. This responsibility was transferred to the police department in 1872 and remained there until a separate agency was created in 1881.[6]

A more onerous function for policemen in these years was their obligation to offer lodging in the stationhouses for homeless vagrants. This duty had been protested by police authorities as one that "undermined the health of the police by exposing them to disease through foul people and air." The New York police succeeded in

see Shane Stevens, "The 'Rat Packs' of New York," *New York Times Magazine,* Nov. 28, 1971.

[4] *Police Systems in the United States* (2d ed.; New York: Harper & Row, 1960), p. 15.

[5] *Varieties of Police Behavior* (Cambridge, Mass.: Harvard University Press, 1968), pp. 4-5.

[6] James F. Richardson, *The New York Police: Colonial Times to 1901* (New York: Oxford University Press, 1970), pp. 225-226.

divesting themselves of this job by 1896. Providing food and shelter
for the homeless was also a controversial function of the Boston
department.[7]

When police organization became a subject for scrutiny in the
first decades of this century, most scholars perceived that the police
had two basic functions (in addition to the miscellaneous service
duties), which seemed to call for contradictory priorities and methods.
Fuld differentiated these functions as the preventive and the punitive,
which in America "are seldom differentiated, although logically the
duties of the police easily lend themselves to such a classification."
By "preventive" police work, Fuld meant the job of "maintaining
a regular patrol of the streets day and night, ... enforcing the city
ordinances," and "the regulation of street traffic"—basically the patrol
and traffic functions of the modern police force. In "punitive" police
work, policemen had to "ferret out criminals and assist the courts
in convicting them," or what we would describe as the crime fighting
function. This side of policing, Fuld noted, was most efficient in
countries where people's freedom was weak, as in Russia or France.
In the United State, punitive operations were "least efficient." He
attributed this to the fact that "the most effective detective work
requires a constant interference with personal liberty, which is
repugnant to American ideas."[8]

Wilson, in his modern analysis of American police styles, described these two functions as order maintenance and law enforcement. The first involved those discretionary areas that Fuld labeled
"preventive" whereas the second dealt with issues of guilt or inno-
cence.[9] This analysis minimizes the political implications of the law
enforcement function that Fuld had described as punitive and which
he had found most clearly in the police states of Europe.

FOREIGN MODELS

Behind these early explorations of police function was the premise
that there was a substantial similarity of function that remained
constant despite national variations. Police reformers at the beginning

[7] *Ibid.*, pp. 264-266; Roger Lane, *Policing the City: Boston 1822-1885*
(Cambridge, Mass.: Harvard University Press, 1967), pp. 191-194, 206.

[8] Leonhard Fuld, *Police Administration: A Critical Study of Police Organisations in the United States and Abroad* (Montclair, N.J.: Patterson
Smith, 1971, reprinted from 1909 ed.), pp. 4-7.

of this century were especially prone to treat American policing as a vastly inferior cut from the same cloth as the police systems of Europe, and they often recommended modifications of American policing based on the more efficient and developed police departments on the continent and in England. Fosdick studied American policing after completing a work on the police agencies of Europe and was melancholy about the contrast between the two. He wrote of the "fundamental divergencies in national conditions, customs, and psychology which pile up obstacles in the way of efficient police work in America almost beyond the conception of the average European official." These divergencies included the greater American heterogeneity, the higher rate of crime, the inefficiency of other agencies in the criminal justice process, the "red tape and technicalities" of the legal structure, and the "weak sentimentality of the community in relation to crime and the criminal."[10]

The most popular model against which American police departments were measured was the London Metropolitan Police, originated by Sir Robert Peel in 1828 and traditionally recognized as the first modern police force. It was the most attractive model for American policing, in part because it did not have the "police state" implications that came to mind when examining the efficient but less democratic police agencies of Europe and Russia. "The English police system," Fuld wrote, "combines in a peculiarly happy manner administrative efficiency with local independence."[11]

This admiration for foreign police models, however, led these scholars to neglect the substantial differences that were present in the development of American policing, which had evolved symbiotically with other urban institutions. American municipal police departments had originally existed as extensions of local political processes. Recent studies of the history of policing in Boston and New York City documented the extent to which these departments were intrinsically involved in the political life of the city, despite superficial similarities with organizational components of the London model.[12]

Fuld made some recognition of this political connection when

[9] *Op. cit.*, pp. 16-17, 85.

[10] Raymond Fosdick, *American Police Systems* (Montclair, N.J.: Patterson Smith, 1969, reprinted from 1920 ed.), pp. 4, 29, 43.

[11] *Op. cit.*, p. 13.

[12] Lane, *op. cit.*; Richardson, *op. cit.*

he said that in the United States the police "are considered by the people as well as in the practical administration of politics and government as municipal officers. ...." He also understood that the concept of a centralized police agency was a European import rather than a native American institution and that metropolitan or regional policing resulted either from the desire to secure more effective law enforcement in selected areas like liquor laws or for partisan advantage in the continuous struggle between cities and the state legislatures.[13]

There were other basic differences between the London police style and that which developed in the United States. Miller, in comparing the origins of the London and the New York City police departments, pointed out that each had to be defined in accord with public demands that the maintenance of order be limited by protection of civil liberties.[14] However, the two cities used very different strategies to achieve this end. In London, the police were established as professionals, in the broad sense of the word, who were subordinate to the rule of law. New York City police were established as amateurs subject to the rule of the people, that is, the local electorate.

The London police, in Miller's analysis, identified themselves with that country's legal system rather than with popular changes within the city. They sought to maintain an impartial stance in relation to the law, a posture that enabled them to retain support from middle-class Londoners who feared that the police would become repressive agents of the aristocracy. In this manner, traditional English hostility against the establishment of a standing semimilitary force was overcome. Although the "bobbies" themselves were primarily working-class recruits, their enforcement of the law protected the interests of middle-class persons who could not afford private security measures and had been easy targets of urban violence. The emphasis on due process also permitted the police to resist efforts by reformers to interfere with working-class life styles.

While espousing many of the features of the London police, American departments became closely identified with the local political leadership, whether it was Tammany in New York City or Cox in Cincinnati. This was a system that obviously invited corruption,

[13] *Op. cit.*, pp. 15-16.
[14] Wilbur Miller, "Police and the Rule of Law: London and New York City, 1830-1870," presented at the Annual Conference of the American Historical Association, December 1971.

just as the local political leadership was corrupt, and in many cities the police department deserved the bad reputation that has come down to the present in police histories. However, the police structure itself had a basis in some of the most enduring characteristics of American democracy: faith in home rule, in the "community's effective sovereignty,"[15] in the belief in amateur public servants.[16] The impartial stance of London's department was rejected on the grounds that any intelligent citizen with the "face validity" of local identity could perform official public duties, including police duties. The resolution of problems of discretion, of selection of priorities, would flow so naturally from community values that they need not even be articulated.

The broad discretion that this implied became a key issue where unpopular laws were concerned. It was relatively easy for an organized pressure group to push for state or local legislation restricting Sunday drinking, gambling, and other practices, but enforcement was exceedingly lax. Fosdick called this "one of the most embarrassing phases of the whole question of law enforcement."[17] Policemen could hardly be blamed for this situation of nonenforcement, but they were constantly exposed to charges of corruption and compromise by those groups who supported a particular law or ordinance. This became a significant component in the movement to reform municipal policing in the early twentieth century because it coincided with what Haller has described as "a series of concerted campaigns to eliminate vice and the white slave trade from American cities" in the period from 1905 to 1915.[18]

Haller's study of the history of the Chicago Police Department further supported the thesis that political activities were central, not peripheral, to the policeman's job.[19] He asserted that the police were

[15] Robert Wiebe, *The Search for Order: 1877-1920* (New York: Hill & Wang, 1967), p. 44.

[16] Frederick C. Mosher, *Democracy and the Public Service* (New York: Oxford University Press, 1968), pp. 61-62.

[17] *Op. cit.*, pp. 48-49.

[18] Mark Haller, "Theories of Criminal Violence and Their Impact on the Criminal Justice System," in *Crimes of Violence*, National Commission on the Causes and Prevention of Violence, vol. 13 (Washington, D.C.: U.S. Government Printing Office, 1969), p. 1331.

[19] "Civic Reformers and Police Leadership: Chicago, 1905-1935," in *Police in Urban Society*, ed. Harlan Hahn (Beverly Hills, Ca.: Sage Publications, 1971).

an integral part of the political process of the city and, while functioning in that context, had a different set of attitudes from that of the reformer. Moral reformers of this era, because of their attitudes and the nature of their reforms, were barred from machine politics. They rejected not merely the machine and its allies, including the police, but also the values that underlay them. In attacking the police for failing to enforce vice laws, they were implicitly attacking the large constituencies that did not wish these laws enforced.

The police thus forfeited the legitimacy that middle-class support could give them and were ultimately no stronger than the authority of the ruling political faction. The mandate of the police, being shakily rooted in the law, was transitory, and Vollmer's drive for professionalism was based in part on the desire to free policing from the insecurity and "degradation" of political servitude.

Confronted with these differences between American and foreign policing, scholars like Fuld, Fosdick, and Vollmer tended to overestimate the extent to which importation of foreign models could solve the problems of American policing. They perceived little in the nineteenth-century American police tradition that was worth saving and established the imported models as their ideal.

THE I.A.C.P.

American municipal policing had always been parochial in outlook, but toward the end of the nineteenth century, police leaders recognized their occupational identity by forming an association called the National Chiefs of Police Union.[20] The organizational meeting, held in 1893, raised issues of uniformity of police selection, cooperation among cities in apprehending and detaining criminals, residence requirements for policemen, whether the police should control boards of health, and so forth.

The pressures that police chiefs were facing in their cities were apparent in their comments at the union's meetings. In 1895 the president, Chief W. S. Seavey of Omaha, reported that interest in the union was increasing "not withstanding the alleged 'moral wave' which has swept over our country, having for its object the disruption of the police departments in many instances." He emphasized that

[20] The *Proceedings of the Annual Conventions of the I.A.C.P.* have been reprinted by Arno Press and the *New York Times* (New York, 1971).

police leaders should be "nonpartisan in their political ideas."[21] There was frequent reference by police chiefs in their speeches to the difficulty of doing their job in a department "run especially on political lines."[22]

Most of the union's early efforts were directed toward setting up cooperation among departments through the mechanical aids of telegraphy and the Bertillon system of identification and through the removal of obstructing variations in criminal codes and procedures. In 1897 the president asserted that police departments were "entirely different organizations to what they were several years ago" and defined the "first duty of an efficient policeman" as crime prevention. "We do not look for, we do not expect, the support of the criminal classes," he said, alluding to groups in the society that challenged law and order.[23]

Starting in 1901, Major Richard Sylvester of Washington, D.C., was elected president and remained in that position for an unprecedented thirteen years; his department was cited as a model for others to follow. An important factor in Sylvester's prominence was his strategic position "at the hub of the United States, where we want to make an effort to federalize the National Bureau of Identification," the association's cooperative agency.[24]

Sylvester's first full year in office, in 1902, saw a significant change in emphasis in the association. President McKinley had been assassinated in 1901, "at a period of the country's prosperity, and at a time when that statesman had attained the zenith of his greatness. . . ." The deed "awakened the heads of the police to a realization beyond doubt that there exists in this country an element antagonistic to the state which renders and receives aid from a like element abroad." Because foreign police leaders expressed willingness to help "stay the progress of the disease," the association was made international[25] and assumed its present name, the International Association of Chiefs of Police.

Many of the subjects that occupied the association from this time were later to become familiar components of professional polic-

[21] *Proceedings* for 1895, pp. 8-9.
[22] *Proceedings* for 1896, p. 12.
[23] *Proceedings* for 1897, pp. 8-9.
[24] *Proceedings* for 1901, pp. 40-41.
[25] *Proceedings* for 1902, pp. 5-6.

ing: the promise of science in improving police methods, problems of police selection, and the continuing issue of "the powerful pressure of political and other influences" upon the chief.[26] This last factor occasionally became a matter of some embarrassment to the association, when a convention site would hurriedly be changed because the "host" chief had lost his job. As Sylvester lamented in 1905, "we were recently informed that the wheels of the political engine had crushed the fondest hopes" of the San Francisco chief.[27]

Until his retirement in 1914, Sylvester was a strong influence in the I.A.C.P. and on the thinking of police leaders in the nation. He had entered the Washington, D.C., department after a career in newspaper journalism. He favored central government involvement in policing and often referred to policemen as "civilian soldiers." In addition to his efforts to increase police efficiency, Sylvester urged the police to form closer relationships with reform groups. "I am of the belief that in some cities there is a feeling against the policeman because himself and his work is not properly understood."[28]

Sylvester's speeches before the association often combined the themes mentioned above of promise and threat: "The world has attained its highest evolution in recent years," he said in one paragraph, citing the "wireless telegraphy, aerial transportation, the moving picture, and the time explosive bomb," and in the next paragraph he warned against "nefarious schemes and ugly callings"— like the "Black Hand"—brought to the nation by immigrants.[29]

However, there had not yet been formed an accepted ideology of a skilled professional who must be trained to meet the threat. Chief Griffin of Kansas City delivered a paper, also in 1911, that quoted extensively from Fuld's recent book on police administration and affirmed Fuld's conclusion that policing was basically a miscellaneous function. Griffin noted that a policeman walking a day beat "usually has little to do" and should, "upon blanks furnished for the purpose, report all defects in streets and sidewalks," and so forth. He described the policeman as "the strong arm raised to assist all other municipal departments."[30]

[26] *Proceedings* for 1904, p. 29.
[27] *Proceedings* for 1905, p. 15.
[28] *Proceedings* for 1901, p. 45.
[29] *Proceedings* for 1911, pp. 11-12.
[30] *Ibid.*, pp. 104-107.

CIVIC AND MORAL REFORMERS

The reform movements that often plagued police departments during these years were composed of a combination of groups with different goals, whose separate efforts were ascendant and sometimes coincided at different periods. There were, however, two distinct and frequently conflicting strains of reform that may be labeled "civic" and "moral" reform.[31] The moral reformers concentrated upon the evils of poor social conditions and vices like liquor, prostitution, and gambling and advocated a policy of active meddling into the lives of those groups—usually the lower and working classes—whom they saw as harboring or being misled by these evils. Mennel's work on juvenile delinquency and Platt's study of the motivation of reformers who established the juvenile courts and other delinquency control measures provided major examples of the effect these groups had upon the criminal justice system.[32]

During Vollmer's early career, from 1905 to 1920, moral reformers provided the noisiest pressure for changes in policing through their attack upon police involvement in political corruption and upon lax enforcement of vice laws. In some cities, competing vice operations were owned by different political factions, and the police were rightly accused of enforcing the vice laws in accordance with political affiliation.[33]

But although he was active in suppressing open and illegal vice in Berkeley, Vollmer shared with other police practitioners a skeptical attitude toward the use of law enforcement to curb vice. His own beliefs were much more attuned to the goals of the civil reformers, who gained increasing prominence during the 1920s. They were more

---

[31] Material in this section is largely dependent on the analysis of Haller, in his "Civic Reformers and Police Leadership," *op. cit.*, and "Theories of Criminal Violence," *op. cit.* Haller has used the term "civic reform" to include both these goals. For our purposes, "moral reform" connotes the goal of active vice suppression and the amelioration of problems like poor schools, dilapidated housing, high disease rates, etc.; "civic reform" connotes the general improvement of police services for business and middle-class interests.

[32] Robert M. Mennel, *Thorns and Thistles* (Hanover, N.H.: The University Press of New England, 1973); and Anthony M. Platt, *The Child Savers* (Chicago: University of Chicago Press, 1969).

[33] See Haller, "Civic Reformers and Police Leadership," *op. cit.*, p. 40.

interested in improving the efficiency of police departments in their role as protectors of personal safety and property.

Civic reformers brought Vollmer to Los Angeles in 1923 and in other cities set up the crime commissions that paid for his surveys of police departments. A National Crime Commission was established in 1925 and was described by one participant as "the crusade of organized business against organized crime."[34] Haller has suggested that in Chicago the business-minded civic reformers were more successful in the long run in their efforts to reform the Chicago police than were the moral reformers. The Chicago Crime Commission, which operated from 1919 to 1935, concentrated on police administrative reform and "ignored almost completely the corrupt relationships that the police had with vice and gambling. . . ."[35]

These two strains of reform, working sometimes in conjunction and sometimes at odds with each other, formed two categories of thought that were used to approach the problems of police organization. Although they differed in the intensity of their disapproval of political corruption, both moral and civic reformers agreed that a healthy police department was one that was as far removed as possible from direct control by elected officials.[36]

From a contemporary perspective, it is perhaps difficult to appreciate the fervor and controversy that surrounded the issue of vice law enforcement. It was a period of national transition, and much of the battle between opposing ethnic and class groups was waged over forms of behavior that we now label "victimless crimes," a description that would be incomprehensible to a middle-class citizen of early twentieth-century America who was alarmed by the turmoil in the cities and the erosion of "traditional" American values. "To reformers, the immigrants were the source of municipal squalor and corruption."[37]

The police were deeply involved in this controversy, although there were few police leaders who did not understand the futility of enforcing codes of behavior or who did not resent the existence of laws that placed the police in an untenable discretionary situation.

[34] "Theories of Criminal Violence," *op. cit.*, p. 1334.

[35] "Civic Reformers and Police Leadership," *op. cit.*, pp. 45-47.

[36] Joseph R. Gusfield, *Symbolic Crusade* (Urbana: University of Illinois Press, 1963) examined the activities of one important group of moral reformers, the temperance movement.

[37] John Higham, *Strangers in the Land* (New York: Atheneum, 1972), p. 77.

2 EARLY YEARS IN BERKELEY

> This man is a Berkeley Product and *Known of Berkeley men.*
> He is ambitious to make a record for himself and the record
> will be good.
>
> *Berkeley Advocate* endorses Vollmer
> for marshal, April 6, 1905

REFORM IN CALIFORNIA

In California, citizens in the Progressive movement had very specific
targets to attack in their fight for good government. More than in
any other state, California officials had permitted a few large businesses to dominate public and economic life. Every area of the state
was run for the profit and convenience of big business, most notably
the Southern Pacific Railroad.[1] Confronted with this skein of corruption, California reformers crusaded for clean government and rejected
the class implications of traditional municipal politics, scorning both
the excesses of big business and the clamor of labor interests.
California's present system of nonpartisan local elections is the legacy
of this era, one of many governmental reforms implemented by the
Progressives.

Both San Francisco and Oakland, neighboring cities to Berkeley,
were run by corrupt machine politicians in 1906. At the turn of the
century, San Francisco was the scene of an intense political battle,
where "muckraking newspapermen joined forces with business and
professional groups to battle one of the most ruthless and graft-ridden
city machines in the state," that of Boss Ruef, who had gained control
of the city's political apparatus in 1901.[2] The reformers initiated court

[1] George Mowry, *The California Progressives* (Chicago: Quadrangle
Paperback, 1963, reprinted from 1951 ed.), pp. 10-22.

[2] John Owens, Edmond Costantini, and Louis Weschler, *California Politics
and Parties* (New York: Macmillan, 1970), p. 33.

17

action against the machine in a series of trials that took place between 1906 and 1909. Dramatic press coverage of these events, which triggered a "statewide campaign against political corruption," dominated the front pages of the newspapers.[3] The police department in San Francisco received publicity for sharing in the graft and vice protection of the machine.[4]

Berkeley citizens were intensely aware of the political climate in their region although their town had less public corruption than its neighbors. It was a reformist, temperance-minded community of 20,000, where churches and theological schools carried some weight in public affairs and where the academic and professional people living around the University of California campus lent an atmosphere of intellectual accomplishment to the town.[5]

Although Berkeley was a quieter town than others in 1905, gambling and opium dens operated openly in the Chinese district and were largely ignored by Marshal Charles Kerns, who claimed that his small force of three deputies was inadequate to police the growing town. Another complaint against Kerns was his failure to enforce the "one-mile law," proscribing the sale of alcoholic beverages within a one-mile radius of the university campus. (Berkeley became a totally dry town in 1907.)[6]

The position of marshal was, on a much smaller scale, similar to that of sheriff. In Berkeley the marshal stood for election every two years and was responsible for performing a loosely organized body of services.[7] The marshal's job became the key race in the April 1905 election, when a slate of reform Republican candidates was successful in winning all offices. The *Berkeley Daily Gazette* headlined its post-election story: "Overwhelming Defeat of Marshal Kerns— Victory for Good Town Government."[8]

Vollmer was well known in Berkeley and had been approached by several leading citizens to run for marshal. His most important

[3] *Ibid.*

[4] Walter Bean, *Boss Ruef's San Francisco* (Berkeley: University of California Press, 1952), pp. 46-47.

[5] See W.P.A. Writers Program, *Berkeley: The First 75 Years* (Berkeley, Ca.: The Gillick Press, 1941).

[6] See the news stories in the *Berkeley Advocate*, February to April 1905.

[7] See the discussion of marshals in Bruce Smith, *Police Systems in the United States* (2d ed.; New York: Harper & Bros., 1960), p. 85.

[8] April 10, 1905.

sponsor was Friend Richardson, editor of the *Gazette*, later governor
of California from 1922 to 1926.[9] Another was the local postmaster,
George C. Schmidt, for whom Vollmer had worked the previous five
years as a letter carrier.[10] Vollmer's campaign was aggressively
championed by the *Gazette*, which editorialized: "Gus Vollmer is a
man of mental acumen and sagacity, and his service in the army
has particularly fitted him for the job of hunting down and apprehending criminals. ... He has the physical strength to cope with
any criminal, and besides he has the necessary grit and courage."[11]
Vollmer campaigned hard throughout the town and won election
by a margin of three to one.[12] He took office on April 15, 1905, at
the age of twenty-nine.

VOLLMER'S BACKGROUND

Although the local paper asserted that he was "a Berkeley
Product," Vollmer was born in New Orleans on March 7, 1876.[13] His
German-born parents, John and Philippine Vollmer, owned a grocery
store there. John Vollmer died of a heart attack when his son was
eight years old, and the mother subsequently sold the store and took
the family—August, an older adopted sister, and a younger brother—to
her home village in Germany to live. Vollmer attended German
schools for two years until his mother became dissatisfied with life
in Germany and brought the family back to New Orleans.

Vollmer enrolled at the New Orleans Academy, a vocational
school, where he took a course in bookkeeping, typing, and shorthand.
This was the only formal education he received past the grade school

[9] Alfred Parker, *Crime Fighter: August Vollmer* (New York: Macmillan,
1961), pp. 38ff.

[10] Mary Johnson, *The City of Berkeley: A History* (typewritten ms. in
Berkeley Main Library dated April 1942), p. 117; interview with Willard
E. Schmidt, *August Vollmer: Pioneer in Police Professionalism* (interviews
conducted by Jane Howard Robinson, Regional Oral History Office, Bancroft
Library, University of California, Berkeley, 1972), p. 1.

[11] Quoted in Parker, *op. cit.*, pp. 41-42.

[12] *Berkeley Daily Gazette*, April 10, 1905.

[13] Information on the life of August Vollmer and the development of the
Berkeley Police Department is taken in part from the following sources:
interviews in *August Vollmer: Pioneer in Police Professionalism, op. cit.*;
Albert Deutsch, *The Trouble with Cops* (New York: Crown Publishers, 1955);
and Parker, *op. cit.*

level. Shortly thereafter, the family relocated to San Francisco because, according to Vollmer, his mother was disturbed by the level of violence and crime in New Orleans. In later years Vollmer recalled that in the same train they took to San Francisco rode the widow of New Orleans' police chief David Hennessy, who had allegedly been murdered by the "Black Hand."

This was the incident that produced the first acknowledgment by American law enforcement that there was a secret society among Italian immigrants called the "Mafia." Nineteen Italians, including a nine-year-old boy, were arrested for the murder but acquitted in a jury trial. Angry vigilantes, led by the "best citizens in the community," killed ten of the defendants after breaking into the jail where they were held.[14]

After living in San Francisco for a short time, the Vollmers moved to a house in Berkeley, on Bonita Street, in 1891. August Vollmer worked at miscellaneous jobs in the Bay Area until, in 1894 at the age of eighteen, he opened a coal and feed store with a friend in Berkeley. He was also active in the formation of the North Berkeley Volunteer Fire Department and was awarded the town's Fireman Medal in 1897.[15] When the Spanish-American War broke out in 1898, Vollmer sold his share of the business to his partner and enlisted in the army. He spent a year in the Philippines, arriving there shortly before the Spanish were expelled from Manila. His company did police duty in Manila and also served on river patrols against rebel guerrilla forces. Vollmer admired the organizational skills of the professional army corps and frequently referred to his army experiences in later years in the context of discussing police operational strategy.[16]

When he returned to Berkeley, Vollmer took a job as a letter carrier. He did not appear to have any strong ambitions for the future, but within the small town he was well known and popular. Vollmer was by nature gregarious, interested in music and ideas, and was readily accepted into the circle of creative young people who lived in Berkeley. Indeed, he had a striking gift for friendship that was apparent throughout his personal and professional life. In 1904 he even acquired a reputation for heroism, after jumping aboard a

[14] James D. Horan, *The Pinkertons* (New York: Crown Publishers, 1967), pp. 418-441.

[15] See Appendix, Chronology of the Career of August Vollmer.

[16] Parker, *op. cit.*, p. 142.

runaway railroad flatcar and stopping it just before it could crash into a local commuter train. The newspaper carried a picture of "Gustave Vollmer" in his postal uniform and reported: "Vollmer is very modest about his performance and refuses to admit that he did anything unusual, despite the fact that his friends are congratulating him on his bravery."[17] The incident doubtless contributed to his reputation for "grit and courage" that the *Gazette* mentioned during the 1905 election.

Except for his year in the army, nothing in Vollmer's background of work or education bore any relation to traditional police work although in those days there was little concern about the substantive aspects of the job. However, he was well qualified in political terms, in the sense that he shared the values of those community leaders who wanted to upgrade police protection in Berkeley.

Whatever his motivation for making a bid for the job, Vollmer quickly became fascinated with police work and directed his creative energies toward improving it. He developed the cop's love for interesting crimes and criminals and began a lifetime of voracious reading about crime, social science, police organization, and government problems. In 1907 he ran successfully for reelection. The year 1909 was a turning point in Berkeley when a new charter was adopted that instituted a mayor-council form of government and changed the marshal into an appointive chief of police.[18] Vollmer received the appointment and remained chief for twenty-three years until 1932.

EARLY INNOVATIONS

Years later in a letter to an associate, Vollmer described his early years of police work in Berkeley: "It was a constant battle and there never was an occasion in the first few years when I had any more than a bare majority of the [city] council. It was fight every day and fight every night. In retrospect I count these the most valuable years of my life, although I can't recall when I have ever suffered so much mental torture as I did during those first few years of police service."[19]

There is no doubt that Vollmer confronted opposition and apathy

[17] Unidentified newspaper clipping, Vollmer Collection, Bancroft Library, University of California, Berkeley.

[18] Johnson, *op. cit.*, p. 120.

[19] Letter dated Jan. 20, 1931, to Mr. Cletus Howell. Vollmer Collection.

in his attempts to modernize the marshal's department. But there were also several factors that worked in his favor. When he took over the department, it was small, and he had campaigned on the basis of an increase in the number of deputies. He had strong support from the community leaders who had backed his election and from the local newspapers. Finally, Berkeley was a sufficiently prosperous town to pay for the reforms that Vollmer made, and several times he initiated and campaigned for specific bond issues to finance improvements. The first was a $25,000 bond issue that was approved in 1906 to install an electric signal alarm system in the streets.[20]

Berkeley's status as a university town was of special importance and marked the character of the new department throughout its development. Vollmer had friends on the faculty and was impressed by the perspective that they could bring to police problems. Vollmer's contacts with the university community were often responsible for the direction he took in police reform.

Two weeks after the election, Berkeley's board of trustees appointed six full-time police deputies to begin service on May 1, 1905, at a salary of $70.00 a month.[21] From this time through the end of 1906, Vollmer introduced several modernizing techniques into the department which, although superseded by later technology, encapsulated some of his basic ideas about effective law enforcement.

First, he put his force of deputies on bicycles for greater mobility and speed in answering calls. This was not the first time that bicycles had been used by an American police department—New York City was using them around 1885[22]—but it was the first instance of beat patrolmen using them for regular rounds as well as for dispatching purposes.

Second, he installed an electric alarm system similar to one that was being used in a privately patrolled section of Los Angeles. It consisted of red lights placed in the center of key intersections that flashed in a code to patrolling officers. The alarm system had two effects: It reduced the response time to distress calls, and it increased the control of headquarters over men out on the beat. If an officer did not answer an alarm within a certain period of time, he was

[20] Parker, *op. cit.*, pp. 57-58.
[21] Johnson, *op. cit.*, p. 120.
[22] James F. Richardson, *The New York Police: Colonial Times to 1901* (New York: Oxford University Press, 1970), p. 263.

required to submit a written report stating the reasons for his failure to do so.[23]

Third, Vollmer set up an efficient system of police records through the efforts of Officer Clarence D. Lee, who, before entering police work, had been secretary of a San Francisco business.[24] Lee's methodical business skills were responsible for the success of many of Vollmer's early managerial reforms. The value of well-kept police records was a central theme in Vollmer's policing, and he later lobbied aggressively for state and national records bureaus.

Finally, Vollmer was the first American police administrator to adopt the *modus operandi* system, first devised by English constable L. W. Atcherley.[25] Lee and Vollmer simplified Atcherley's system by reducing the complex categories of information used into more workable sets of data. This was the sort of technique that led some police officers to accuse Vollmer of being too "theoretical" in his approach to crime solving.[26] Traditional American police work did not concern itself with the "nature" of the criminal, nor did it analyze similarities between crimes in any systematic way, although experienced investigators may have done so on an individual basis. The introduction of *modus operandi* into the Berkeley department was early evidence of Vollmer's interest in the use of scientific techniques to solve crime problems.

Almost exactly one year after Vollmer took office as marshal, the San Francisco region was struck by the great earthquake and fire of April 1906. "[E]ven nature," he said later, "seemed to conspire to make my administration difficult."[27] Although Berkeley suffered only minor damage, it and other East Bay cities were inundated by thousands of refugees who crossed the Bay on ferries to escape the fires in San Francisco.[28] Within a few days there were at least 15,000 refugees in Berkeley; some estimates range as high as 50,000.[29]

[23] Interview with William F. Dean, *August Vollmer: Pioneer in Police Professionalism, op. cit.*, p. 4.

[24] Interview with Willard E. Schmidt, *op. cit.*, pp. 2-3.

[25] August Vollmer, "Revision of the Atcherley *Modus Operandi* System," *Journal of the American Institute of Criminal Law and Criminology*, 10 (1919): 229.

[26] Parker, *op. cit.*, p. 145.

[27] Letter dated Jan. 20, 1931, to Mr. Cletus Howell, *op. cit.*

[28] W.P.A. Writers Program, *op. cit.*, pp. 83-86.

[29] Deutsch, *op. cit.*, p. 116.

A number of homeless people stayed with friends and relatives, but a large majority was housed in tents throughout the city, primarily on the university grounds.

Vollmer advertised in the *Gazette* for veterans of the Spanish-American War to assist him and eventually deputized over a thousand citizens to keep order in the camps and manage the distribution of supplies. He said later that there was an impression among the refugees that martial law was in effect under his direction, a rumor that he felt worked in his favor. Food hoarding or stealing was the most serious problem in the camps. He once ordered a deputy who had apprehended several thieves to "take them out and shoot them," a bluff he was restrained from carrying out by others present who interceded for them.[30]

Although Vollmer and his small department were faced with many immediate problems after the earthquake, the real significance of the event for Berkeley was an overnight doubling of population that drastically altered the scope of municipal services. Many people returned to San Francisco after a few weeks, but enough stayed in Berkeley to boost its population to around 50,000. Along with the people, Berkeley received a considerable impetus to its commercial growth: "It is not Christian to seek advantage in another's misfortune, but there is nothing to be ashamed of in profiting by such misfortune if it comes unsought. There is no doubt but the greatest impulse that has come in Berkeley's history toward its commercial development has had its beginning in the destruction of the business section of San Francisco by earthquake and fire on April 18th."[31]

It was this influx of population and capital that helped make Berkeley a "boom town" during those years, leading to its incorporation in 1909 and a broad range of civic improvements in which the police department shared. In effect, Vollmer was required to turn his force of marshals into an urban police department within a short span of time.

From the start, Vollmer received considerable coverage in the newspapers, which characterized him as the "boy marshal" and carried stories about his bicycle patrols and other reforms. Most of the coverage was sympathetic, especially in Berkeley. Vollmer was skillful in publicizing his department and fully appreciated the value of

[30] *Ibid.*, p. 117.

[31] Warren Cheney, "Commercial Berkeley," *Sunset Magazine*, December 1906, quoted in W.P.A. Writers Program, *op. cit.*, pp. 83-84.

favorable newspaper publicity. As a result, the Berkeley department received the notice of a wider audience than would be expected for such a small city force. It was the beginning of Vollmer's national reputation.

In 1906, police chiefs in the state organized the California Police Chiefs Association, and in the following year Vollmer was elected president.[32] It is likely that he was involved in organizing the association although he had only been in policing for a year. From the start, Vollmer had become conscious of the way in which local political boundaries interfered with law enforcement. Even in the first decade of the century, before automobiles became a significant factor, Berkeley was considerably less isolated than it had been as a small town. Since 1903 the Key Route train line had been running in connection with the ferries that crossed the Bay, and demand was great enough to support a twenty-minute schedule during commute hours. These were people who lived in the East Bay and worked in San Francisco. The fare was only 10¢ a ride or $3.00 for a monthly ticket.[33]

This ease of transportation was good for Berkeley in terms of growth and prosperity but brought with it the problems of neighboring cities. Vollmer analyzed Berkeley's crime problems: "the nearness of two large cities which harbor many criminals," the fact that "two transcontinental main lines run through the town," the "ease with which it is possible to hide here, and the many different routes that may be taken to leave after having committed a crime."[34] Berkeley's residents were prosperous enough to attract professional criminals, who took advantage of the new transportation lines to commit burglaries in Berkeley homes when the owners were across the Bay in San Francisco.

There were almost no formal mechanisms for police departments to share information about criminal activity until the state set up a Bureau of Criminal Identification in 1905, but this agency was designed to serve major state agencies and did little to assist local police. It operated in part out of San Quentin prison, which distributed information about incoming and discharged prisoners.[35] Neighboring

[32] See Appendix, Chronology of the Career of August Vollmer.
[33] W.P.A. Writers Program, *op. cit.*, p. 83.
[34] *Ibid.*, p. 127.
[35] Interview with Thomas P. Hunter, *August Vollmer: Pioneer in Police Professionalism, op. cit.*, p. 2.

police departments shared material relevant to criminal identification and unsolved crimes, but in the absence of a central repository for such data, the procedures were awkward.

Despite Vollmer's preoccupation with the job of reorganizing his own department, he had become acutely aware during these early years of the larger factors that influenced police efficiency. He began working with the California Police Chiefs Association to establish a central records bureau in California and was soon speaking in favor of a national records bureau. He appreciated the importance of information in police work, and within his own department it was evident that the successful use of techniques like *modus operandi* depended upon the amount and quality of data that were available.

SCHOOLING FOR POLICEMEN

In 1908 Vollmer began the Berkeley Police School, the first formal training for police officers in this country, and a prototype for later in-service and academic programs in California. Most departments did not even have informal police training at this time. An Oakland policeman who joined the force around the turn of the century, after appointment by his city councilman, was assigned to a beat, given a revolver and nightstick, and told to "keep law and order in that district on foot, of course."[36] These conditions prevailed in most American police departments at the time that Vollmer entered policing, and it was the image of the "dumb cop," who obtained his position through political patronage, that Vollmer was most determined to change.

The police school at Berkeley was attended by deputy marshals while off duty. Classes in police methods were taught by Vollmer and Walter Petersen, at that time Chief of Inspectors in Oakland. Petersen, who later became chief of the Oakland department, was credited by Vollmer with giving him much practical advice during his early years as marshal. Other instructors were drawn from the university: William Helms, a professor in the parasitology department, taught sanitation law, made more relevant by a bubonic plague scare in the area; and Professor A. M. Kidd of the law school taught criminal evidence. First aid and photography were among the technical subjects presented.[37]

[36] Deutsch, *op. cit.*, p. 226.
[37] Parker, *op. cit.*, pp. 81-83.

Vollmer frequently cited a dramatic case that occurred in 1907 as awakening his interest in the importance of scientific crime investigation.[38] A man had been found dead by poison, and the coroner's jury ruled that the death was a suicide. Vollmer was dissatisfied and gathered evidence that convinced him that the death was a homicide. His friend Dr. Jacques Leob, a biology professor at the university, gave him facts about the poison which indicated that the victim could not have taken it himself and his body found in the position it was. Vollmer brought his findings to the county grand jury and was extremely disappointed to have the original verdict of suicide upheld—not because the reasoning of the investigation was wrong but because the initial police investigation had been too careless in establishing the basic facts at the scene to support a verdict of homicide.

This single case summed up for Vollmer the frustrations he felt in using old-fashioned methods of police investigation, and he began to appreciate the complexities of obtaining criminal evidence that would stand up in court. He had also failed several times in trying to gather evidence against gambling houses during his first years as marshal because witnesses were almost impossible to obtain and the operations of the houses were designed to obscure physical evidence at any sign of police presence.

When he looked into the subject, Vollmer was awed by the amount of technical information that could be used in crime investigation. In 1916 he began an association with Dr. Albert Schneider, a professor in the pharmacy school who had been doing work in forensic medicine. Schneider agreed to give lectures in the police school and later that year joined the department as a full-time criminologist.[39] He established at Berkeley the first scientific crime laboratory in the United States, which in turn brought attention to Vollmer's department as a center of modern police work.

Vollmer's interest in schools for police officers grew over the years into a conviction that police studies was an appropriate subject for higher education. The police school remained primarily technical in orientation, despite its expansion into some related academic subjects.[40] In 1916 Vollmer established a formal relationship with the

[38] This story is related in both Parker, *op. cit.*, pp. 72-76; and Deutsch, *op. cit.*, pp. 117-118.

[39] Parker, *op. cit.*, pp. 88-89.

[40] See August Vollmer and Albert Schneider, "The School for Police as

University of California by commencing a series of summer session courses which he taught almost continuously until 1931. These courses were attended by both working policemen and university students and covered such topics as the problems of crime, methods of police investigation, medical examination of criminals and delinquents, and legal relations involved in criminology.[41] He gained a reputation as an impressive lecturer and sometimes livened his classes by inviting professional criminals in to give guest lectures on the tricks of their trades. This university program began a process of cross-fertilization between the academic community and the police department which established both as forces uniquely involved in the development of education for policemen.

Vollmer and Schneider co-authored an article on the Berkeley Police School in 1916 which appeared in the *Journal of Criminal Law and Criminology*.[42] In the same issue an editorial from a Chicago newspaper was reprinted entitled "Police Work a Profession, Not a Job," which urged the Chicago Police Department to upgrade its program of police training. The writer of the editorial cited Berkeley as the leader in developing police training programs through the joint efforts of the police department and the University of California. Vollmer was quoted as comparing police training with that of lawyers and doctors: "Inefficiency and all the ills that follow in its wake may be expected until this professional status is recognized by the public and prepared for by the press."[43]

This journal, based at Northwestern University, was published by the American Institute of Criminal Law and Criminology. Vollmer became active in the institute in 1917, perhaps drawn into it by his friendship with Professor Kidd, who was the California representative for new members in that year. As in other organizations, Vollmer assumed a leadership role; he was elected president of the California chapter in 1917 and became national vice president the following year. He was also named an associate editor of the journal in 1917. In subsequent years he published articles on criminal identification, *modus operandi*, police selection procedures, crime prevention, and

Planned at Berkeley," *Journal of the American Institute of Criminal Law and Criminology*, 7 (1917).

[41] Allen Gammage, *Police Training in the United States* (Springfield, Ill.: Chas. C Thomas, 1963), p. 61.

[42] *Op. cit.*

[43] *Ibid.*, 622-624.

other topics. Vollmer was a capable writer, and the interdisciplinary journal was a natural forum for his ideas about professional policing.

In 1915 Vollmer was invited to San Diego, which had had scandals in its government and police department, to do a survey. This was the first of at least a dozen major police surveys that Vollmer did during his career, plus many more that were done by junior officers under his supervision. Vollmer's reactions to the situations he found in these cities were often privately caustic and seemed to renew his determination to keep his career anchored in Berkeley, where he had built a position that was virtually impervious to manipulation. He had a strong, personal aversion to the political corruption and interference with policing that he found in these cities.

In a 1917 letter to an officer who was working in San Diego, Vollmer described the mayor of that city as "pin-headed" and a "psychopathic idiot" and urged: "Do not hesitate to go after him roughshod, now that he has come out into the open, and have all your friends do likewise, because you are absolutely right and there is no reason in the world why you should lie down and be a good dog just because he wants you to."[44]

In his reports Vollmer stressed the importance of protecting the police chief from capricious hiring and firing and made recommendations for internal reforms in procedure and techniques. However, because he believed that lasting reform was outside the control of department officials, he urged his contacts in these cities to be aggressive organizers of public opinion for their cause, especially through the press and sympathetic citizen groups and service clubs. His correspondence over the years with former Berkeley policemen in other cities was full of practical advice and a cynical appreciation of the obstacles that they faced in countering political harrassment.

Through this decade, Vollmer continued to work with the California Police Chiefs Association for a state records agency.[45] Police leaders had become unified in their fight for the agency after the legislature failed in 1909 even to vote appropriations to continue then existing but inadequate operations. Vollmer became a "veritable one-man lobby" for the proposed agency, for which bills were introduced in 1913 and 1915. His own draft bill called for a "Bureau of Police and Criminal Identification of the State of California," and

[44] Letter dated June 28, 1917, to Mr. W. A. Gabrielson, Vollmer Collection.
[45] Material on this subject is taken from John P. Kenney, *The California Police* (Springfield, Ill.: Chas. C Thomas, 1964), pp. 22, 48-53.

he attempted to include provisions for state policing in the final bill. Both these bills passed the legislature but were vetoed by Governor Hiram Johnson, apparently under pressure from labor groups who feared that the agency would develop into the state police organization that Vollmer envisioned. This was a period during which state police in other areas were being used for the open and frequently brutal suppression of strikes and labor organizing.

The agency was finally approved in 1917 as the State Bureau of Criminal Identification and Investigation, "the latter word added to encompass a broader scope of activities as had been conceived by August Vollmer and other law enforcement officials." Kenney has suggested that labor interests supported the 1917 bill after being assured by police leaders that the agency would not evolve into a state police organization. The new governor was William D. Stephens, and Vollmer urged him to sign the bill by "setting forth the argument that it would be helpful in catching spies and subversives, inasmuch as World War I was under way at the time." Vollmer served as president of the first board of managers of the new agency, and a Berkeley policeman, C. S. Morrill, was appointed superintendent.

THE PUZZLE OF CRIMINALITY

By 1919 Vollmer had established himself as an innovative police administrator and a crusader for new approaches to the problem of criminality. He immersed himself in a reading program that exposed him to ideas from multiple disciplines, which he believed could be incorporated into modern policing.

Professor Loeb, an early friend who influenced Vollmer in his first decision to run for marshal, introduced him to the possibilities of scientific analysis in crime investigation and suggested readings in both the natural and social sciences. Loeb first drew Vollmer's attention to the works of the Austrian criminologist Hans Gross (1847-1915), who was trained as a lawyer and is regarded as the originator of criminalistics.[46] His works on criminal investigation and psychology were strongly empirical and were intended to acquaint those who were involved in the determination of guilt with the technical, scientific, and psychological data that were relevant to

[46] See Roland Grassberger, "Hans Gross," in Hermann Mannheim, ed., *Pioneers in Criminology* (Montclair, N.J.: Patterson Smith, 1972).

criminal activity. *Criminal Psychology*, published in 1897, was an atheoretical compendium of knowledge about human nature and deviant behavior that was based on Gross' years as an examining justice in the Austrian provinces. In the early years of this century, Gross' work was the most extensive treatment of problems in crime investigation that was available. Vollmer was strongly influenced by Gross and recommended his books on the reading lists for police training programs.

In his enthusiasm for new ideas and the academic aspects of criminology, however, Vollmer was less critical than when he worked with the practical side of police administration. He was developing his ideas at a time when theories about crime tended to look for single factors as causes of delinquent behavior.

Since about 1910, American criminologists had been looking for new theories about crime causation to replace the discredited premises of criminal anthropology.[47] It had become evident to serious researchers that a cataloguing of "stigmata" and cranial dimensions was inadequate to explain the etiology of criminal behavior. But most criminologists retained a belief that a single, identifiable factor could be isolated that would account for specific behavior patterns. The measuring ground moved from the delinquent's body to his mind, and intelligence tests were used to identify those persons who were mentally "defective." A whole new class of citizens—and aliens—labeled "feebleminded" was born. Feeblemindedness was accepted as a significant typology, and asylums were considered the answer to protecting society from contamination until careful research after the First World War indicated that more complex variables were involved.

This was the theoretical climate within which Vollmer was trying to educate himself about crime causation. Many of his actions and writings in this area reflected the belief that if only certain isolable factors were known, criminals could be identified and either treated or restrained, depending upon the nature of their defect. Criminal psychology was, in this view, almost a puzzle, which well-trained policemen could use their skills to solve in conjunction with social scientists. The best example of this was an early case—in 1908—in which fires were set in homes in a certain district of Berkeley. Vollmer

[47] See Mark Haller, *Eugenics* (New Brunswick: Rutgers University Press, 1963), pp. 115-117.

turned to Gross' book and came up with this answer: Find an adolescent, mentally retarded male youth, visiting in this district but whose home is many miles away. Such a youth was located by the police, and he admitted to the arsons.[48]

As a working policeman, Vollmer had a valuable empirical sense of the ins and outs of criminal behavior, but he was consistently weak when he sought to generalize from his experiences into theory. It was a weakness that was shared by many criminologists and social scientists in that day and would be unimportant in this context except as it affected Vollmer's vision of the work that a professional policeman could do. Just as criminological researchers erred in assigning crime to a single cause, Vollmer erred in believing that policemen could become specialists in crime causation. He knew that policemen developed a good working knowledge of the patterns of behavior that they might expect from particular individuals or classes of individuals, but he was overly confident that they could apply this knowledge toward a deeper understanding of crime itself. Vollmer's ideal of professionalism in policing, at its more abstract level of understanding, included the belief that the profession could make significant progress in solving social problems.

Modern theory denies the likelihood that criminal behavior may be traced to a single factor, and some social scientists question the existence of a category of activity that may be labeled "criminal" apart from the accretions of culture, politics, and legalism.[49] Most of Vollmer's early writings on this subject—and, to a significant degree, his 1949 work *The Criminal*—must be evaluated in light of his roots in the earlier period.

Similarly, "discoveries" from psychology and psychiatry were sometimes used by Vollmer to explain the behavior of people in political movements, as seen in a 1921 newspaper clipping entitled "I.W.W. Mentally Twisted, Says Chief of Police Vollmer."[50] The article cited a study done by Vollmer and his long-term associate, psychiatrist Dr. Jau Don Ball; it was described as "a scientific study of persons classified within the three distinct groupings [of] I.W.W.ism, Bolshevism, and parlor Socialism," which "constitute a type of

[48] This story is told in Parker, *op. cit.*, pp. 78-79; and in Vollmer, *The Criminal* (Brooklyn: The Foundation Press, 1949), pp. 297-298).

[49] See Austin T. Turk, *Criminality and Legal Order* (Chicago: Rand McNally, 1969).

[50] Unidentified clipping in Vollmer Collection, dated internally as 1921.

insanity in the paranoica group," Vollmer was quoted as saying. He characterized the leaders in these movements as "a definite, well-recognized type of mentally twisted people" and the followers as "generally of the feebleminded type." "Defects in both cases are weakness of judgment, weakness of understanding, impervious to reason, touchy, senseless action, chronic grumbling." The article concluded that Vollmer planned to campaign for a nationwide program of institutions to care for these individuals. (No further evidence of such a program has been found.)

The example is given here to illustrate Vollmer's uncritical acceptance of social science theories, not to imply that he had a violent reaction against political radicalism. As will be shown later, Vollmer was unusually tolerant in his political and social views and frequently defended the civil liberties of others at the expense of his own reputation. Despite the political hysterics of the era from which the article dates, Vollmer's files and letters contain only passing reference to the issue of political subversives, and there is no indication that he participated in any significant way with government actions against radicals. His overriding point of view in politics and government was one of skepticism.

CRIME PREVENTION

As fascinating as dramatic crimes and criminals were, however, most of the "crime fighting" done by the police was directed against the more mundane forms of delinquency. Vollmer's ideas about the work that policemen could do in day-to-day crime prevention were of more importance than his views about the theories of deviant behavior. He envisioned the policeman as an integral part of a community-wide alliance that would map strategies to deal with the "pre-delinquency" problem and to alleviate the obvious social and psychological bases of it.

This type of preventive work was being accepted by progressive police leaders as a responsibility of the force. Woods, who had been head of the New York City Police Department, wrote in 1918 about the police function as work that would "diminish the supply" of criminals rather than merely make their work more difficult.[51]

[51] Arthur Woods, *Crime Prevention* (Princeton: Princeton University Press, 1918), pp. 29-32.

One of Vollmer's early statements about policing and social action to prevent crime was an article entitled "The Policeman as a Social Worker," which was published in a police journal in 1919 after being delivered before a meeting of the International Association of Chiefs of Police.[52] In it he described his view of the policeman as the "ultimate" crime fighter, as one who understood crime and worked to prevent its occurrence.

He declared that "dependency, criminality, and industrial unrest have a common origin" and staked out as part of the policeman's job the obligation to deal with it. To accomplish a task of such magnitude, it was necessary that "we raise the educational and intellectual standard of our police departments, elevate the position of the policeman to that of a profession, eliminate politics entirely from the force, and secure the people's confidence, sympathy, respect, and cooperation." It was a clear statement of Vollmer's essential philosophy about the policeman and his job.

He believed that the policeman who knew the people on his beat was in an excellent position to identify problems and refer them to other community professionals for treatment. As examples he cited three case histories which reflected the wisdom of the day about crime causation. The first was that of a young girl arrested for stealing who was taken to a "psychopathic clinic" and found to be "somewhat retarded mentally." Experts believed that "adenoids and enlarged tonsils might be responsible for the defect." The second case was a boy arrested for burglary who was judged to be normal and was sent to relatives in the country for rehabilitation. The third case was a middle-aged man who was arrested for burglary and subsequently found to be a "medical problem ... a neurasthenic with morbid impulses; the result of overwork and financial worries."[53]

In Berkeley, in 1915, Vollmer organized a junior police program of several hundred boys who were given military drills and involved in community projects.[54] Vollmer was sympathetic to young people and what he called their "excess animal spirit" and always stressed the importance of good relations between police officers and the youth on their beat.

Dr. Jau Don Ball was a major influence on Vollmer's thinking about crime prevention; together they worked on problems of police

[52] *The Policeman's News*, June 1919.
[53] *Ibid.*, pp. 12-42.
[54] *Saginaw* (Michigan) *Daily News*, Nov. 16, 1915, in Vollmer Collection.

selection and on developing ways of identifying children who might become delinquent as they grew up. The principal result of this latter effort was an extensive study conducted at Berkeley's Hawthorne Elementary School in 1919 that was intended to predict juvenile delinquency through the use of various "mental, physical, and social examinations." A wide array of local social agencies cooperated with the police department in administering the tests to 200 children.[55]

It was, in effect, a pilot project for the kind of continuing involvement in crime prevention that Vollmer urged police departments to undertake in their communities. There is no evidence that the results of this study were used in any systematic way in terms of intervening in the lives of those who were considered pre-delinquent, but Vollmer referred to the study frequently in following years as an illustration of constructive and professional police work to deter crime. He discussed the results of the study in *The Criminal*.[56]

A more lasting result of the study, at least in Berkeley, was the creation of a coordinating council to deal with juvenile problems in the community. Representatives from the police, the schools, and health, welfare, and recreation departments began an "alliance" designed to unify the efforts of the separate agencies in preventing delinquency.[57] Vollmer believed strongly in the principle of involving the police in a continuing, interagency effort that would increase the effectiveness of community resources; the council was not merely to establish policies but to handle specific problems as they arose.

The success of Berkeley's coordinating council during these years was difficult to emulate in other settings. Vollmer commented in a 1936 letter that the "Berkeley plan has operated without any constitution or bylaws and is based upon the principle that a formalized coordinating council would defeat its purpose. The members of the Council voluntarily meet once a week without a definite program for the purpose of discussing the problems as they arise."[58]

The informality of the group and the dedication of the members were essential. Obvious problems would arise in a large city where each of the agencies involved was a substantial bureaucracy in itself, hampered by internal formalism from exercising flexibility at an

[55] Deutsch, *op. cit.*, p. 136.
[56] *Op. cit.*, pp. 417-423.
[57] Deutsch, *op. cit.*, p. 136.
[58] Letter dated Feb. 15, 1936, to Mr. S. P. Robbins, in Vollmer Collection.

interagency level. In his letter Vollmer mentioned a small city where the workings of the council had been disrupted by political factionalism. The Berkeley Council, however, was a good example of the work that could be accomplished by committed participants who were functioning within a supportive community setting.

In the years from 1905 to 1919, Vollmer developed a respected police department in Berkeley and acquired a national reputation as a spokesman for the improvement of policing through separation from politics, education for officers, and the adoption of efficient new techniques. Policemen were to comprise a new profession—to be equally proficient as crime fighters and social workers. Their status in the community would be a reflection of their role as protectors and counselors. For this job, every available technical and academic resource would be used, and competent police leaders would be free to function without "illegitimate" interference from political factions.

Vollmer's gospel about turning policemen into professionals was a welcome message to many progressive citizens in the cities where the police were either embarrassingly incompetent or openly corrupt. It appeared to offer a way out of the cycle of bad government leading to bad, even abusive policing. In effect, it could short-circuit the process of decline by creating an independent, nonpartisan police force, where salaries would be high enough to discourage graft and where the policemen would be honorable and skillful. Moral reformers, disturbed by the shifts in urban life, were more inclined to trust a police department that was detached from political factions of dubious character. Civic reformers hoped that professional policing would be more effective in controlling property crime. And as his best example, Vollmer consistently drew attention to the operations of the Berkeley department, where, under his leadership, it had actually managed to reduce crime and control the police budget at the same time. It was a compelling message.

PREVENTS RUNAWAY CAR FROM CRASHING INTO BERKELEY TRAIN

Gustave Vollmer.

Letter Carrier Gustave Vollmer Leaps Aboard Moving Car and Applies Brakes Just as Passenger Train Pulls Into Station

BERKELEY, Jan. 16.—The bravery and quick action of Gustave Vollmer, a letter carrier in the Berkeley postoffice department, prevented what might have been a serious railroad wreck shortly after noon today. He jumped aboard a runaway flat-car at the Berkeley station and, exerting all his strength, put on the brakes and brought the car to a standstill just as the Berkeley local, laden with passengers from San Francisco pulled into the station. The runaway car was on a siding, and had it not been stopped in time would have run down the incline to the main track and have crashed into the Berkeley local.

The flat-car, loaded with heavy bricks, broke loose from the rest of the train unnoticed by the freight crew. As it started bystanders tried to stop it by throwing bricks on the rails in front. It got beyond their control, however, as Vollmer came along. Realizing the danger of a collision with the local train, loaded with passengers, he swung aboard the car and effectually applied the brakes.

Vollmer is very modest about his performance and refuses to admit that he did anything unusual, despite the fact that his friends are congratulating him on his bravery.

The freight yards of the Southern Pacific are located in the heart of the town, adjoining the Berkeley station, and the switching trains are a constant menace to life.

Some time ago the railroad officials announced their intention of moving the yards to the gore at Adeline street and Shattuck avenue, but so far the removal has not taken place.

Vollmer in his postman's uniform in 1904, the year before his election as Berkeley marshal. The picture appeared in a local newspaper article detailing Vollmer's role in stopping a runaway railway car. He was incorrectly identified as "Gustave," from his nickname, "Gus." Courtesy Bancroft Library.

The Berkeley Police Department in a 1908 photograph taken on the south corner of Allston Way and Shattuck Ave. The department was divided into two platoons, each working a 12-hour shift. Lighter, khaki uniforms are worn by the day shift, black uniforms by the night shift. Courtesy Berkeley Police Department.

Front row, left to right: Bart Campbell; Ira Tidd; Geo. Kohler; Wm. Wright; Jos. Leonard; Officer McCabe; Jack Le Strange; Louis Richardson. Middle row: Inspector H. Jamison; Sgt. A. S. J. Woods; Sgt. C. D. Lee; Sgt. Thos. Woolley. Rear row: H. Nelson; Tom Jones; Jim Davis; C. Miller; Ed Barff; Frank Waterbury; C. McClintock; O. A. Kelley; Ira Bohrer.

A photograph of the department taken in 1929 or 1930, taken in the rear of City Hall. City Manager John N. Edy and Vollmer stand at the left. The department was housed in the basement of City Hall until the new headquarters were built in 1939. Courtesy Berkeley Police Department.

Front row, from far left: John N. Edy, City Manager; August Vollmer; J. A. Greening; Frank Swain; Chas. Ipsen; Wm. A. Gabrielson; Ernest Terry; Jack Fisher; Chas. Penning; Bert Fraser; Floyd Wise; H. P. Lee; Harold Schulze; V. A. Leonard; Ralph Pidgeon; Harry Hoggard. Second row (all identications uncerrain): Don Simpson; Albert Coffey; Patrick O'Keeffe; (next three unknown); Wm. E. Baird; Ray Foreaker; Tom Maybell; (unknown); E. C. Johnson.

A course in microscopy in the Berkeley Police School, 1915. Standing is Dr. Albert Schneider, the instructor. Vollmer is at the far left and C. D. Lee, who helped to set up Berkeley's early records system and M.O. procedures, is seated fourth from the left. Courtesy Bancroft Library.

Seated, left to right: August Vollmer; Capt. A. S. J. Woods; Sgt. Oscar Purzker; Capt. C. D. Lee; Capt. Walter Johnson; Frank Ingersoll, Superintendent of Records; Sgt. Charles Becker. Standing: Dr. Albert Schneider.

Published Daily Except Sunday at
Record Building, 612 Wall Street

FRIDAY, SEPTEMBER 28, 1923

THEY DON'T WISH HIM ANY BAD LUCK, BUT—

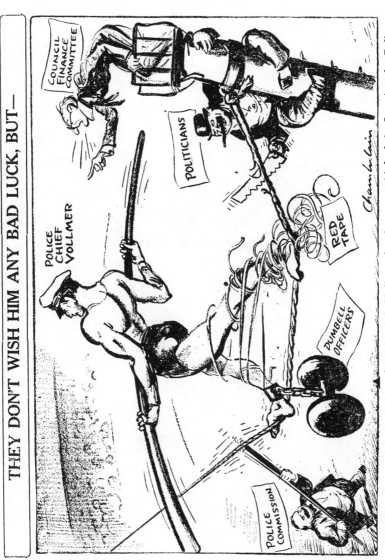

A political cartoonist's depiction of the hazards Vollmer faced as new chief of the Los Angeles Police Department in 1923. Courtesy Bancroft Library.

3 THE BERKELEY DEPARTMENT

Why should not the cream of the nation be perfectly willing
to devote their lives to the cause of service, providing that
service is dignified, socialized, and professionalized.

Vollmer, letter to Jack Greening (1930)

THE DEATH OF POLICE UNIONISM

In September 1919, a year after the Berkeley department began a
drive to recruit college students, Boston had a police strike over the
right to affiliate with the American Federation of Labor. This strike,
the culmination of a widespread effort among policemen to use the
labor movement to improve working conditions, led to the dismissal
of over three-quarters of the men in the department.[1]

The rapid growth of unionism was the major employment trend
of this era. Many police departments had already organized social
groups and benevolent associations, which reflected the growing
occupational consciousness of policemen and were useful in improving
morale. However, the pressures under which policemen worked at
this time were inaccessible to solution by organizations that did not
have formal authority to bargain with public officials.

The justice of the policeman's grievances was undeniable. An
article in the *National Police Journal* a few months before the strike
commented sympathetically upon the growth of police unions: "Since
the municipalities won't listen to his just plea, [the policeman] is
compelled to take matters in his own hands. Unions have always
fought for the rights of labor. So the policeman naturally turns for
help in that direction."[2]

[1] Material on this subject is largely taken from Richard Lyons, "The
Boston Police Strike of 1919," *New England Quarterly*, June 1947, p. 151.
For a short history of the police labor movement, see Hervey A. Juris and
Peter Feuille, *Police Unionism* (Lexington, Mass.: D. C. Heath, 1973).

[2] Jack Larric, "The Police and Labor Unions," *National Police Journal*,

The American Federation of Labor, led by Samuel Gompers, had begun to grant police charters in 1919 and by September of that year granted charters to thirty-three municipal police departments. Boston's application included by far the greatest number of members —975 out of a force of 1,544 men. The next largest proposed police union was 135 members from St. Paul, Minnesota.

The earliest opposition to police unions had come not from public officials but from within the A.F. of L. When a group of special police in Cleveland petitioned in 1897 for a charter, the A.F. of L. went on record opposing police unions on the grounds that "it is not within the province of the trade union movement to especially organize policemen, no more than to organize militiamen, as both policemen and militiamen are often controlled by forces inimical to the labor movement."[3] Since that time, however, various police groups had appealed to the federation for membership until policy was finally reversed early in 1919.

In an article written thirty years later, Richard Lyons showed that the move of Boston policemen to unionize was born of desperation, after attempts to improve working conditions and to raise salaries through ordinary political channels had failed. Since 1913 salaries had risen an average of 18 percent, but the cost of living had risen 86 percent. Policemen were required to live in the stationhouses while on duty; conditions there had been investigated and judged to be unsanitary as early as 1909, but the city made no attempt to improve them. During this same period efforts were being made to enforce antisaloon legislation, thus depriving policemen of an informal source of income—payoffs from saloon owners—that had supplemented their meager wages for years.[4]

Formal application for a charter was made to the A.F. of L. on August 10 by the members of the Boston Social Club, the police fraternal organization, and it was granted the next day. Members of the department who attended a meeting called by the police association voted unanimously to affiliate. The police commissioner responded by bringing charges against nineteen police union leaders for violating new regulations—enacted for the occasion—that prohi-

3, no. 5 (1919): 15.

[3] Quoted in M. W. Aussieker, Jr., *Police Collective Bargaining* (Chicago: Public Personnel Association, 1969), p. 1.

[4] Andrew Sinclair, *Prohibition: The Era of Excess* (Boston: Little, Brown, 1962), p. 263.

bited affiliation with outside organizations. As the situation worsened, an official citizens' committee recommended a compromise that required the police to give up their A.F. of L. affiliation but recognized their right to have a departmental union and specified that no action would be taken against the union leadership.

This compromise was acceptable to the policemen but was rejected by the commissioner, who proceeded to suspend the nineteen defendants from duty. It was this rejection that precipitated the strike, which was approved by an 1,134 to 2 vote of the membership. Governor Coolidge soon called out the entire State Guard, who combined with volunteer units to comprise a force of over 7,000 men, after disorders broke out in the city and which local officials were not prepared to handle. All the striking policemen, comprising three-fourths of the department, were subsequently dismissed, and police unionism was dead in Boston and in every other American city for years to come.

Since the Boston strike, police leaders and the public have tended to regard police unionism as inherently illegitimate. (The strike provoked Coolidge's well-remembered statement, in reply to an appeal by Samuel Gompers: "There is no right to strike against the public safety by anybody, anywhere, anytime.") An element in this attitude was the fear that a unionized police would not act impartially during labor disputes.[5] To most officials, however, "impartiality" meant enforcing the law against strikers, as labor leaders were well aware and which accounted for their earlier opposition to police unions.

Thoughtful observers at the time recognized that the efforts to unionize were based on real grievances and that suppression of unionism would have to be followed by an alternate system of redress. Raymond Fosdick wrote a year later: "[The community] cannot strip them of the weapons of defense which other workers have, and at the same time ignore their just claims because they are pressed merely by argument."[6]

Vollmer was scornful of the idea of police unions. A month after the strike, he wrote: "My opinion is that it would be just as sensible for policemen to join forces with the Bankers, Producers, or Manufacturers Associations as to become identified with the American Federa-

[5] Elmer Graper, *American Police Administration* (Montclair, N.J.: Patterson Smith, 1969, reprinted from 1921 ed.), p. 319.

[6] *American Police Systems* (Montclair, N.J.: Patterson Smith, 1969, reprinted from 1920 ed.), p. 321.

tion of Labor." He recognized that working conditions were poor in most police departments, but he considered it "utterly impossible" that they should affiliate with an organization designed to deal merely with conditions of employment. They should organize into "one national body" that would work aggressively to "present their claims to the public and their legislative representatives."[7]

CIVIL SERVICE REFORM

There was one alternative model for reform that was available for policing at the time; that was the civil service movement. This reform was based on the premise that political patronage was the greatest evil in government. "By denying politicians the spoils of office, the argument ran, civil service would drive out the parasites and leave only a pure, frugal government behind."[8]

The thrust of this reform, embodied in the Pendleton Act of 1883, was clearly moral, not merely designed to increase efficiency in public service. "Its prime objective is to remove from American politics the degrading influence of the patronage system."[9] Wiebe commented on the faith of the age with simplistic solutions: "Because most reformers conceived the world as an orderly affair where societies, like planets, normally functioned according to rational laws, they had customarily looked for that one gear askew, that one fundamental rule violated, as an explanation for America's troubles."[10] Mosher referred to civil service reform as "essentially a negative movement designed to stamp out a system which was 'a disgrace to republican institutions'—to eradicate evil."[11]

Nowhere was the "disgrace" of the spoils system more obvious to reformers than in municipal policing, which in many cities operated as the coercive arm of the dominant political faction. Although civil service was obviously more applicable to some branches of government than others, it was commonly believed that it would be the best

[7] From " 'No Divided Allegiance,' Say Chiefs," *Policeman's News*, October 1919, p. 49.

[8] Robert Wiebe, *The Search for Order: 1877-1920* (New York: Hill and Wang, 1967), pp. 60-61.

[9] From the 1891 report of the Civil Service Commission, as quoted in Wiebe, *ibid.*, p. 61.

[10] *Ibid.*, p. 62.

[11] Frederick Mosher, *Democracy and the Public Service* (New York: Oxford University Press, 1968), p. 65; internal quotation from Dorman B. Eaton's *Civil Service Reform in Great Britain*, 1879.

method for removing the evil of politics from law enforcement. This development was accepted reluctantly by police leaders because they had little to suggest in its place, but they were quick to note its deficiencies in a police context. Graper wrote halfheartedly of the benefits that civil service had brought to policing by saying that it had "at least eliminated, where honestly applied, the grosser abuses which almost invariably prevail where the system is not in force." He also spoke of the more constructive aspects of civil service in efficiency rating and standardizing duties, grades, and salaries but conceded: "Unfortunately, these improvements have not been reflected in police service to such an extent as in some other fields of municipal administration." In the crucial matter of civil service competitive examinations, Graper called them "a very defective basis for making promotions in the police service."[12]

During this same period, Raymond Fosdick, while granting the need to protect police chiefs from capricious political interference, said that civil service "has too often proved a bulwark for incompetence and neglect. . . . Too often, too, it has served as a respectable cloak for political juggling, defeating its own purpose, and bringing the whole cause of reform into disrepute."[13]

Other areas of government service employed the civil service system with varying success and were able to introduce more constructive reforms in conjunction with it (the U.S. Post Office, for example). Policing, however, more subtly intertwined with politics, less clearly defined in function, and more difficult to evaluate in terms of performance, found at best a minimum protection from abuse through civil service. This has been recognized for years and was a concern to police administrators at the time that Vollmer was working in Berkeley.

"GOLDEN YEARS"

In striking contrast with the turmoil and demoralization of the Boston police, the Berkeley department was entering a period that one enthusiastic commentator labeled the "Golden Years" of the Berkeley police.[14] At this time Berkeley was almost a laboratory for

[12] Graper, op. cit., pp. 70-71, 81.
[13] American Police Systems, op. cit., p. 260.
[14] Albert Deutsch, The Trouble with Cops (New York: Crown Publishers, 1955), pp. 122-123.

new ideas about police techniques and personnel. The department was well established, and Vollmer had become a nationally known police leader.

The Berkeley success came from Vollmer's ability to find good men to be police officers and to use their talents well. Professional policing began when Vollmer decided, rightly or wrongly, that the police officer required significantly special skills to do his job, skills that could not be learned on the beat by a recruit who was indifferent to the "higher purposes" of policing. That is why it was inconceivable to him that a policeman should become identified with workingmen whose sense of occupational purpose extended only so far as a decent wage and adequate conditions on the job.

Vollmer's almost visionary belief in the goal of the professional policeman marked his actions and writings over the years. "Surely the Army offers no such opportunities for contributing to the welfare of the nation, and yet men unhesitatingly spend their lives preparing for army service," he wrote in 1930.[15]

As his ideas about the education needed for policing grew more ambitious, Vollmer decided that it was fruitless for the department itself to attempt to provide college-level material that established institutions were better able to teach. Although the police department ran a progressive training program of its own, he came to believe that the ideal police officer would be one who had already received academic training before he was recruited and who could be trained in the technical aspects of police work after joining the force.

To test out this idea, the Berkeley department began to recruit college students to serve as patrolmen on the force. This was the beginning of Berkeley's "college cops," a program for which the department and Vollmer received nationwide attention; a number of Vollmer's most talented protégés entered the department at this time.

The challenge of meeting high entrance standards was doubtless an important factor in attracting college students into an occupation with a traditionally low status. The department had begun to use the Army Alpha intelligence test, which was developed during the war, to screen applicants. Dr. Ball, who had performed similar work with the U.S. Army, was retained to administer the tests and pass

[15] Letter dated Oct. 15, 1930, to Acting Chief Jack Greening, Vollmer Collection, Bancroft Library, University of California, Berkeley.

upon the fitness of applicants for the job. During the decade of the 1920s the instrument became a common screening device among other police departments, but average scores varied widely. Berkeley's average score of 149 points was far above that of the Detroit department, where sergeants averaged only 55 points.[16]

Another inducement to young college men was the high pay that the department offered. In 1923 salaries were $170 a month plus $30 for the use of the officer's car. (Officers used their own cars on duty until the 1950s, when a fleet of police vehicles was purchased.) There was also a mild recession during the early 1920s that forced some students to find jobs while attending college and that had contracted the job market for those who were graduating.[17]

By 1921, according to one estimate, there were a dozen college-student policemen out of a force of twenty-eight or thirty men.[18] As was expected, some of the students left the department after they graduated and entered other careers. But many decided to stay in police work and, under further tutelage from Vollmer, became influential on their own in police administration and related fields. These "college cops" included George Brereton, police educator and former head of the California Bureau of Criminal Identification and Investigation; William F. Dean, general in the U.S. Army; Walter A. Gordon, former governor of the Virgin Islands and head of the California Adult Authority; V. A. Leonard, police educator and writer; and John D. Holstrom, chief of the Berkeley department from 1944 to 1960 and later a police consultant.

The most influential of this new generation of police leaders was O. W. Wilson. After four years in the Berkeley department, Wilson left in 1925 at Vollmer's urging to head the department in Fullerton, California, where he encountered much political opposition but began to build a reputation as a progressive police chief. He served as chief of the Wichita, Kansas, department for eleven years, in 1950 headed the new School of Criminology at Berkeley, and then became superintendent of the Chicago police. Although Wilson's philosophy of policing came to differ from that of Vollmer in many ways, Vollmer's

[16] Richard H. Blum, *Police Selection* (Springfield, Ill.: Chas. C Thomas, 1964), p. 99.

[17] Interview with O. W. Wilson and John D. Holstrom, *August Vollmer: Pioneer in Police Professionalism* (interviews conducted by Jane Howard Robinson, Regional Oral History Office, Bancroft Library, University of California, Berkeley, 1972), p. 1.

impact upon his career was far more than that of an inspiring mentor. Wilson said of his book *Police Administration* that it "reflected Vollmer's principles and philosophy and I went through the book thoroughly with him, chapter by chapter, so that I would say that it reflects August Vollmer rather than O. W. Wilson."[19]

Walter Gordon was one of Vollmer's first college recruits and also the first black man to serve on the force. Gordon was well known in Berkeley, having been a star football player at the university, and he entered the department to earn his way through law school. His first assignment was in a white residential neighborhood, where a number of complaints and threats were made against him when he started working. Vollmer refused to reassign him for racial reasons, however, and Gordon was eventually accepted throughout the city. (The 1920 Census gave Berkeley a total population of 56,036, with 911 Japanese, 507 blacks, 337 Chinese, and 115 Mexicans.)[20]

Vollmer recognized Gordon's abilities and urged him to stay in police work, but he left the department after graduation to enter law practice. During this period, Gordon also had contact with Earl Warren, who appointed him to be head of the new Adult Authority when Warren became governor.

It was the basis of Vollmer's success in these years that he was able to recruit men of high caliber into the force who were receptive to his ideals about professional policing. They also saw an opportunity to build successful careers for themselves by following Vollmer's example in other departments. Inevitably, somewhat uneasy relationships developed with neighboring police departments when unflattering comparisons were made between them and Berkeley, and the "college cops" were not warmly received in Oakland or San Francisco. "Two things you didn't say, one was you didn't emphasize you were from Berkeley, and you certainly didn't emphasize that you went to the university. ...."[21]

What was the nature of the work that Vollmer expected of them? A 1921 recruit paraphrased Vollmer's remarks to the new officers:

You're not to judge people; you're just to report what they do wrong.

[18] *Ibid.*, p. 2.

[19] *Ibid.*, p. 4.

[20] Mary Johnson, *The City of Berkeley: A History* (typewritten ms. in the Berkeley Main Library dated April 1942), p. 47A.

[21] Interview with John D. Holstrom, *August Vollmer: Pioneer in Police Professionalism, op. cit.,* p. 18.

Better still, you can prevent people from doing wrong; that's the mission of a policeman. ... I'll admire you more if in the first year you don't make a single arrest. I'm not judging you on arrests. I'm judging you on how many people you keep from doing something wrong. Remember you're almost a father-confessor; you're to listen to people, you're to advise them. ...[22]

He expected each man to be the "chief" of his beat, to bear responsibility for dealing with problems of any nature that came up within the area he patrolled. One officer recalled that a patrolman felt that he had failed in his job if a fire on his beat was spotted and turned in by someone else.[23] He was to work closely with merchants to establish preventive measures and to know the families on his beat well enough to detect delinquency problems or unusual needs.

In other words, in Vollmer's philosophy, the patrolman did not merely work within a professional organization; he was a complete professional in himself, selected through rigorous testing, trained in a progressive police school, and imbued with the ideals of service and efficiency.

It was the philosophy of the generalist in policing, as opposed to the specialized operative who was assigned to a single category of work. Wilson wrote that in Berkeley "the beat officer is responsible for all crimes committed on his beat, and he must clear cases by the arrest of the perpetrator and the recovery of the stolen property. As careful a check is made of clearances by individual patrolmen in Berkeley as was kept of individual detectives in Wichita." Although Berkeley had specialists in criminal investigation, they were not brought into a case unless the patrolman requested their assistance or unless they were led there as a consequence of other investigations in progress. The patrolman was "the fundamental unit responsible for the performance of all phases of police duty regardless of whether it involve crime, vice, juvenile offenders, or traffic."[24]

Vollmer viewed his department as a training ground for police leaders who would proselytize throughout the country for the ideals of professional police service, and he urged his officers to set high

[22] Interview with William F. Dean, *August Vollmer: Pioneer in Police Professionalism, op. cit.*, p. 1.

[23] Interview with Willard E. Schmidt, *ibid.*, p. 21.

[24] Letter dated Dec. 12, 1940, to Mr. Ray Ashworth, Vollmer Collection.

career goals. "One of Vollmer's great attributes," an officer said, "was his extraordinary ability to encourage other people to develop ideas and to develop practices. . . . He had faith in people."[25]

He set high standards for conduct in his own department, and he was strict and severe in maintaining prohibitions against dishonesty and brutality, especially against prisoners. "On force, the rule was very simple. I heard it from him when I was a police recruit. It was that no Berkeley policeman should ever strike any person, particularly a prisoner, except in extreme self-defense; and then he said, if you ever do, you have just resigned. You needn't bother to come in and discuss it, and this one he meant."[26]

In practice this policy may have been moderated, but it was close to being enforced in a literal way. Vollmer personally handled disciplinary matters, and when he was on leave in Chicago in 1929, he instructed the acting chief concerning an officer who had slapped a suspect: "It is my opinion that Inspector S— submit an undated resignation which will be placed in his file and used if he again fails to control his temper on any future occasion."[27]

Police brutality, especially through the use of "third degree" methods, was a prime issue of the day. Vollmer abhorred the widespread use of force within police departments because he felt that it demeaned the police and jeopardized the support they needed in the community. A professional policeman, trained in the law, in criminal psychology, and in scientific investigation, would have no need for such extralegal techniques in order to make his case. Vollmer opposed brutality and intimidation of suspects within the Berkeley department and had a habit of visiting the police jail in the morning to talk with the prisoners to see how they had been treated.[28]

The department also had standards on the use of firearms, although there are no specific examples available to test the workings of the policy. Every Friday, all officers not on duty attended a group meeting to discuss departmental matters. One officer recalled: "If you fired your gun, you would have to get up before the whole group on the Friday Crab Club hour and give the factors on what happened,

---

[25] Interview with John D. Holstrom, *August Vollmer: Pioneer in Police Professionalism, op. cit.,* p. 8.

[26] *Ibid.,* p. 24.

[27] Quoted in letter written to Vollmer on Nov. 20, 1929, by the officer in question, Vollmer Collection.

[28] Interview with Willard E. Schmidt, *op. cit.,* p. 11.

and then there was a decision made by the men from the standpoint of this way or this way; right or wrong."[29]

The Friday meetings, informally called the Crab Club, were a combination gripe and learning session. "For instance, if you had anything against any man in the department, you said it right there in front of him, and after it was over it was forgotten," remembered one officer.[30] During the summer, guest lecturers were brought in, primarily psychiatrists and articulate criminals who shared their expertise with the group. As the department grew larger, these meetings were also a means for exposing new officers to Vollmer's ideas about policing.

Even when Vollmer was absent from Berkeley, he maintained strict and personal control over internal department matters. If problems arose—citizen complaints about police conduct, liquor in the police station, etc.—the acting chief and others in the department wrote him detailed letters giving the facts and soliciting his decision. Civil service was not used as a means of job protection: "No security whatever is offered to the members of the force," Vollmer wrote in 1936, "and tenure is entirely dependent upon their desire to perform their duties. When they cease to do this, their service is terminated." He said that politicians did not interfere with the department because "the character of the men is such that no politician would dare attack them. ... Any attempt to tamper with an official or influence his actions is promptly publicized."[31]

There is no doubt that, compared with other urban areas at the time, Berkeley was a clean town. Vollmer knew that police corruption was almost impossible to avoid in a city where rackets and illegal vice operations flourished. His success in keeping his own department honest stemmed in large measure from his prior success in keeping gambling, prostitution, and bootlegging out of the city and the availability of these services in nearby cities. He had moved against the Chinese gambling establishments very soon after becoming marshal, and they never returned to any significant degree. During Prohibition, Berkeley citizens crossed the city border into Oakland to get their whiskey.[32]

Vollmer was aided in his vice law enforcement by Berkeley's

[29] *Ibid.*, p. 8.
[30] *Ibid.*, p. 9.
[31] Letter dated March 12, 1936, to John W. Anderson, Vollmer Collection.
[32] Interview with John D. Holstrom, *op. cit.*, p. 32.

longstanding support for temperance, and he enjoyed a consensus of public support. At one time, Berkeley was credited with having the highest drunk rate in the country because nearly all cases were reported and handled by the police department.[33] Vollmer opposed the jailing of drunks and always had the police take them to their homes if they had one.[34]

In 1925 the department organized a Crime Prevention Division, for which Vollmer recruited a social worker, Mrs. Elisabeth Lossing, as supervisor. The program became well known as the first attempt to bring professional social workers into a police department on a full-time basis. This division operated essentially as a social welfare agency, focusing on the problems of juveniles (boys under twelve and girls under twenty-one) but including emotional and domestic problems as well. Boys between twelve and twenty-one years of age were supervised under a separate program.

During these years it was the custom in Alameda County, in which Berkeley is located, to send assistant deputy district attorneys to Berkeley to get experience in a good department, and in this way Vollmer began working with Earl Warren, who was assigned to Berkeley in 1923.[35] Vollmer and Warren cooperated on a number of projects, and, after 1925, when Warren was elected district attorney, he involved the Berkeley department in dramatic raids against the bootlegging, prostitution, and gambling interests in neighboring Emeryville and Oakland. Warren routinely used twenty to forty of Vollmer's men to supplement his own small staff in these raids, which at one time involved storming a building that occupied almost a whole city block. The other police departments in the area were considered too closely tied in with the vice operations to be used for support. Dozens of people were arrested and taken to the Berkeley jail for processing.[36] Warren also depended on the Berkeley department for technical assistance, especially in photography, to aid in the difficult process of gathering evidence that would stand up in court.

Warren's ideas about policing were greatly influenced by Vollmer, who inspired him with the need for reform in many areas. They later

[33] Interview with Willard E. Schmidt, *op. cit.*, p. 11.

[34] Deutsch, *op. cit.*, p. 120.

[35] Material on this subject is largely taken from the interview with Willard E. Schmidt, *op. cit.*

[36] Interview with John D. Holstrom, *op. cit.*, p. 33.

worked together to set up education programs in the state and to develop state law enforcement agencies. Their leadership "did much to bring together police and associated groups for the purpose of achieving common objectives. It was largely through their efforts that major programs were conceptualized and initially implemented."[37]

TECHNICAL DEVELOPMENTS

In addition to recruiting college students, the Berkeley department was experimenting in the 1920s with a number of technical innovations. The most controversial of these was the polygraph or "lie detector," which Vollmer and others referred to in subsequent years as the "so-called lie detector," in an effort to meet criticisms that the machine was unable actually to detect falsehoods. The first machine to be used at Berkeley was built by John Larsen,[38] who was trained in physiology at the University of California. Vollmer had asked Larsen to work on the project after reading an article by William Marston of Boston which detailed his own experiments in the area. Leonarde Keeler, who was a student at Berkeley High School at that time, assisted Larsen; after later efforts of his own, Keeler secured the patent for the polygraph and became its best-known specialist. Larsen became a psychiatrist and continued to work in the area of criminality, but he later expressed disappointment in the ways it was being used. ("It is little more than a racket . . . nothing more than a psychological third-degree aimed at extorting confessions as the old physical beatings were. At times I'm sorry I ever had any part in its development.")[39]

The lie detector, although it never attained theoretical respectibility, was to Vollmer a powerful and fascinating tool. It was the best example of what may be called his love of "gadgets," of scientific breakthroughs that he hoped, in the hands of professional police, could make the process of detecting and solving crimes enormously more efficient. Keeler, who moved to Chicago and became the head of a polygraph testing laboratory, worked persistently to refine and

[37] John P. Kenney, *The California Police* (Springfield, Ill.: Chas. C Thomas, 1964), pp. 23-25, 113.

[38] W.P.A. Writers Program, *Berkeley: The First 75 Years* (Berkeley, Ca.: The Gillick Press, 1941), p. 128.

[39] Quoted in Deutsch, *op. cit.*, p. 150.

legitimize the device. He and Vollmer maintained a detailed correspondence about his work and were personally close; Vollmer sometimes referred to Keeler and his wife as "our two adopted children."[40]

In 1921 the street alarm system was replaced by a primitive car radio. The Berkeley department had been using automobiles since 1913 or 1914 and from the start had given automobile allowances to the men in return for the use of their own cars. Vollmer believed that this policy produced greater efficiency than that of maintaining a fleet of city-owned cars because it increased the mobility of the individual officer and cut down on response time when officers were called out on special duty.

The primary reason for the policy, however, was its attraction as a fringe benefit. The automobile was a considerable incentive for recruitment in those days, and the factor of morale was foremost to Vollmer. He countered arguments of economy that the city council and city manager raised by asserting that it would probably require a larger police force to meet existing standards if the incentive of automobile ownership were removed.[41] (Vollmer himself never learned to drive a car.)

Press and Public

Throughout his tenure as police chief, Vollmer was as tireless as a politician in building the good will and support within the community that he believed he needed to maintain a progressive department. He was active in the formation and membership of numerous local betterment groups, continually working to open lines of communication between the police and citizen organizations. He urged his officers to study public speaking and took every opportunity in these years to address groups and solicit their support for police reform. "I have dined for the starving Chinese, I have lunched for the Armenians, I have breakfasted for the unemployed," he wrote to a colleague whom he was encouraging to "go public" on behalf of the department.[42]

Vollmer had unusual skills in rallying public support and discrediting those who opposed him. He had a keen understanding of the

[40] See letters in the Vollmer Collection for the 1930s.

[41] Letter dated June 6, 1933, to J. A. Greening, Vollmer Collection.

[42] Letter dated Jan. 8, 1930, to Acting Chief Jack Greening, Vollmer Collection.

ways in which the press could be used and of the power of a critical press. Several years after becoming chief, he had a policy disagreement with Friend Richardson of the *Gazette*, one of his original supporters, which led to a series of bitter attacks upon him in news stories. The disagreement probably stemmed from Vollmer's rigid enforcement of vice laws, especially against gambling, which some influential citizens wanted to introduce into Berkeley's private clubs. Vollmer maintained a public silence during this time, never attempting to defend himself against the charges, and eventually Richardson initiated a truce. Vollmer referred frequently to this incident when advising his officers on press relations, warning them against fighting unfavorable publicity in the newspapers.[43]

Crime news was a far more prominent topic in the daily newspapers during the years when Vollmer was chief than it is today, and crime reporters were important members of the press. This was also a period in California history when newspapers were a major factor in reform movements. Vollmer established good rapport with the local press by maintaining close relations with editors and reporters and granting unprecedented access to police files.[44]

Full-time reporters were assigned to the Berkeley department from five or six of the local dailies: *San Francisco Chronicle, San Francisco Examiner, Daily News, Berkeley Daily Gazette, Oakland Post Inquirer*, and the *Oakland Tribune*. The last paper, owned by the Knowland family, probably had the greatest political influence. It was represented by Rose Glavinovich, who joined the Berkeley press corps during World War I, its only woman member, and covered the department through the time of Vollmer's death in 1955. She was a close friend to Vollmer, receiving occasional special tips about nonpolice stories (Vollmer was careful to give all newspapers equal access to police news) and serving from time to time as an unofficial policewoman.

During the years when the department was housed in the basement of the municipal building, the press shared the squad room with working police officers. Vollmer allowed reporters to have access to police records so long as they respected notations that requested no publicity on certain stories. The new ideas that were being tried

[43] Interview with John D. Holstrom, *op. cit.*, p. 6.
[44] Material on this subject is largely taken from the interview with Rose Glavinovich, *August Vollmer: Pioneer in Police Professionalism, op. cit.*

out in the department provided continuous good copy for the reporters, and they reciprocated by publicizing them generously. "He just
made the news. He started innovations, and they were news. It just
naturally worked out as news. He was very conscious of the value
of publicity, not as personal publicity, but for the ideas and ideals
he had in police work."[45]

This kind of press support meant a lot to Vollmer in getting
what he wanted from the city government. During the term of the
first city manager of Berkeley, John N. Edy, Vollmer requested a
raise in officers' salaries. He arranged to "plant" a story in the *Tribune*,
with the complicity of Glavinovich, which implied that many "college
cops" were leaving the department because of poor pay. At that time,
students were graduating from college and leaving the department
to take up other career interests, which, contrary to the implication
in the story, was a natural development. Vollmer's program of
recruiting college students as policemen had brought widespread
publicity to the city, and Edy was angered when he read this
distortion. He suspected that it was a concocted story but could not
prevail against the support that Vollmer had secured in the city
council, and the pay raise was granted.[46]

Vollmer's political skills were also evident in the work he did
within professional and citizen groups. To his colleagues he frequently
offered advice on how to turn a situation to their advantage. In a
1929 letter to the mayor of Berkeley, who had written to Vollmer
at Chicago concerning a citizens' law observance committee, Vollmer
replied with extremely detailed instructions on how to organize and
control the committee, how and when to announce it, how to handle
nominations for office, and how to "plant" motions in the audience.[47]
In the 1920s, when several of Vollmer's protégés held executive
positions in other police departments, they often sought advice from
him on ways to overcome political enemies. When Wilson was fighting
his opposition in Wichita, Vollmer wrote him to "prepare a tremendous, concentrated offense plan. ... Your friend will be blasted out
of the community before he realizes what has happened." He advised
to "make no overstatements," to use all of Wilson's men as four-min-
ute or two-minute speakers, and to "see that the entire town is covered
so that no person escapes." He suggested a house canvas to inform

[45] *Ibid.*, p. 3.
[46] *Ibid.*, pp. 1-2.
[47] Letter dated Nov. 6, 1929, to M. B. Driver, Vollmer Collection.

citizens of the issues: "Have the delivery boys of the opposition paper tailed so that you know their subscribers, and during your campaign arrange to have the [sympathetic] *Wichita Eagle* placed in their hands."[48]

Vollmer's "politicking"—both in Berkeley and in the other cities where he worked for short periods—was in the name of professional policing. As his own actions demonstrated, however, Vollmer's policing was not so much detached from politics as it was a separate political entity of its own. In Berkeley, Vollmer was far more than a competent police administrator who had developed good relations with the community. He was an active, dominant force in the life of the city. He turned the police department into an independent power base, which was founded on principles of high integrity and was held to these principles through the force of his personal leadership. He trained his officers to be humanitarian crime fighters and aggressively sought the tools and techniques that would enhance their effectiveness. The scope of such a professional could be limitless, provided he received enough cooperation from citizens and legislators and was freed from partisan political interference.

Given this point of view, it is obvious why Vollmer was opposed to civil service and to unionism. Although he and other police leaders reluctantly accepted civil service reform as a lesser evil than outright political appointment, they believed that it encouraged incompetence and interfered with hiring and promotions. The union movement focused on worker demands, not on the larger issues of training, dedication, and nonpartisanship.

Vollmer was not an armchair criminologist; he put his ideas into practice in Berkeley, and they usually succeeded. Fosdick reported in his *American Police Systems* that for the earlier years between 1908 and 1915, when Berkeley's population increased from 37,000 to 64,000, the value of property stolen decreased 28 percent; during this same period, only five men were added to the force. Fosdick credited this record to "the value of correction and preventive work done by the department in increasing the effectiveness of each member of the organization through improved methods of operation."[49] The test of Vollmer's ideas about professional policing was whether they could succeed in larger, less progressive communities and under different leadership.

[48] Letter dated Sept. 8, 1933, Vollmer Collection.
[49] *Op. cit.*, p. 311.

CENTRALIZED RECORDS

On the national scene, the decade of the 1920s saw a greatly increased concern about efficiency and honesty in policing, and police organizations like the International Association of Chiefs of Police worked within a climate of widespread public criticism of police operations. It was the decade of Prohibition, which put police in the position of enforcing a law that had substantial opposition; and it was the era when problems of traffic control began to assume the dominant role they now play in most urban police departments.

The burgeoning use of automobiles had two important effects on policing. The first was internal; traffic engineering and control was the first major component of modern policing that was well suited for specialization and that encouraged the development of a set of skills that were technical and detached from other aspects of police function.

The second effect was the greater mobility of criminals, which made it difficult for a police department to handle law violations in its own jurisdictions without some assistance from regional or national agencies. Vollmer had articulated this issue when he was marshal and had to apprehend burglars who rode the ferries and trains from San Francisco and Oakland into Berkeley. Automobile use, besides blurring the distinction between neighbors and strangers, greatly aggravated the problem of apprehending suspects. "Migratory criminals are causing an endless amount of trouble," said Vollmer in 1922.[50]

Although the bulk of law violations within an area were perpetrated by locals, Vollmer and his colleagues could point to many dramatic crimes where the multiple jurisdictions of police agencies had hampered detection and arrest. In previous years he had worked to establish a cooperative agency in California and in the 1920s used his prominent position in the I.A.C.P. to lobby for a national records bureau. In 1918 he had been instrumental in forming a special I.A.C.P. committee to persuade the federal government to create a "National Police Bureau."[51] As president of the association in 1922, he argued: "A national bureau of criminal records and crime statistics is imperative, and a workable plan for such a bureau should be devised at

[50] "Aims and Ideals of the Police," *Journal of the American Institute of Criminal Law and Criminology*, 13 (1922): 256.

[51] Deutsch, *op. cit.*, p. 139.

this meeting."[52] The drive for a national bureau had been a key concern of the I.A.C.P. since its formation.

Many local police leaders were suspicious of involving the government in the responsibility for maintaining criminal records. A police bureau had been in operation for twenty years and was supported by contributions from participating agencies. There was concern that police chiefs would lose their control over the organization and that government funding might be cut back or withheld by an unsympathetic administration.

For Vollmer, however, centralization was a major tenet in his philosophy of professional policing. He believed that the combination of first-class personnel and nonpartisan control would be sufficient to prevent the kind of abuses that others feared from the development of a national agency having police functions. In 1925 the I.A.C.P. records became part of the Federal Bureau of Investigation, an agency that combined record keeping with the responsibility for investigation of federal offenses.

Vollmer was clearly in favor of this dual function and considered it appropriate that the agency be more than just a repository for fingerprints, photographs, and other criminal data. When the California records agency had been formed in 1917, he had attempted to have it enacted as a Bureau of Identification and Investigation, but the move had been blocked by state labor interests. The F.B.I., as it developed, reflected many of Vollmer's ideas—an efficient system of records, scientific investigative techniques, high personnel standards, and strong leadership—but it is likely that he was less sympathetic with the agency's ideological overtones.

In 1925 or 1926, J. Edgar Hoover visited the Berkeley department, according to a policeman who was assigned by Vollmer to escort Hoover on a tour of various police departments and state facilities.[53] There is little other evidence of a working relationship between the two, although they exchanged articles and professional materials through a formal correspondence that lasted many years. In a 1933 letter to a former Berkeley policeman who had evidently sought Vollmer's influence in getting Hoover's job, Vollmer replied: "From the fact that I have done everything in my power to assist in keeping

[52] "Aims and Ideals of the Police," op. cit., p. 256.

[53] Interview with Gene B. Woods, August Vollmer: Pioneer in Police Professionalism, op. cit., p. 13.

Hoover as Director of the Bureau, it would be impossible for me to now reverse myself and seek to replace him by another."[54] It is certain that Vollmer supported the principle of maintaining a director who would not be forced to resign because of political changes.

I.A.C.P. PRESIDENCY

In 1922, when Vollmer was president of the I.A.C.P., the annual convention was held in San Francisco. The attending police chiefs were able to visit Berkeley and see the programs that were being tried there. Vollmer's address to the convention, entitled "Aims and Ideals of the Police," outlined several practical reform measures that he urged his colleagues to adopt in their own departments or to press for on a state and national level.[55] First, he discussed recruitment standards and noted that in addition to patrolmen a modern police department must hire "stenographers, filing clerks, typists, photographers, identification and handwriting experts, and other skilled professionals." In support of lateral entry, he said that requiring all police personnel to "start at the bottom and work [their] way up through promotional examinations" had proved to be "wholly inadequate." He continued: "Our work in the community is much more important than is generally believed by the public, and experience has taught us that only the very best human material can render the type of service demanded."

The following are some of the other reforms he recommended in his speech.

1. Increased use of policewomen, especially in the "vast field of pre-delinquency."

2. Police schools for training purposes, wherein the content "may vary slightly in different communities, but the fundamentals in the police school curriculum should be identical in all departments."

3. "Modern equipment, such as signal devices, wireless telephony and telegraphy, automobiles, motorcycles, motorboats, gas bombs, traffic devices, signs and towers, and laboratory apparatus." A common theme in Vollmer's writings, and one that revealed his basic orientation as a crime fighter, was the notion that the police must "compete" with the criminal element, which "uses every new inven-

---

[54] Letter dated May 29, 1933, in the Vollmer Collection.
[55] Material that follows is taken from this speech, *op. cit.*

tion and is usually a league in advance of the police because of that fact." And again: "We must be prepared to meet the criminal with better tools and better brains than he possesses if we hope to command the respect of the community that we serve."

4. Greater emphasis on crime prevention, which he described as "our principal function." In keeping with the theories of the day, he declared: "Human beings are not exempt from biological laws, and the increase of insanity, feeblemindedness, epilepsy, degeneracy, prostitution, and criminality indicates a polluted bloodstream." The policeman has a greater responsibility than others in gaining awareness of these factors and using them to prevent criminal acts. "The public can furnish a thousand different reasons for the crooked act, but the wise policeman remains silent, ventures no opinion, knowing that every factor must be investigated before an intelligent explanation can be given for the individual's failure to conform to the rules made to govern our conduct."

5. The police should contribute their share toward solving the problem of "unnecessary delay and miscarriage of justice in criminal trials."

6. "Uniform national and even international laws, uniform classification of crimes, simplified court procedures, better methods of selecting and promoting properly trained jurists are modern requirements. ..."

7. Police investigators should abandon "trial-and-error" methods of crime solving for more efficient scientific techniques and crime laboratories, enlisting the aid of "microscopists, chemical analysts, medicopsychologists, and handwriting experts."

8. Centralization and improved methods of maintaining police records. "A bureau of records, if properly organized, is the hub of the police wheel."

9. Universities should be petitioned to devote more time to the study of "human behavior, its bearing upon political and social problems, and for the training of practical criminologists, jurists, prosecutors, policemen, and policewomen."

This speech was a good reflection of the components that Vollmer believed were necessary in order to build a professional police organization. His first priority was the selection and training of competent personnel. He believed that the more philosophical problems would be solved naturally if the police were to hire only the best people, to "skim the cream of society" for police work. At the beginning of the speech, Vollmer reviewed the varying functions that were assigned to the police, saying: "Legislative bodies seem somewhat confused at times regarding the purpose and function of the police." It was time for expert policemen to "discuss this fundamental question and prepare a form which may be helpful to legislators in the future." But he never returned to this complex issue of defining the police function.

THE YEAR IN LOS ANGELES

In 1923 Vollmer accepted a one-year job as chief of the Los Angeles Police Department. This was a period when real increases in crime and the additional burden of graft and corruption resulting from the task of enforcing the Volstead Act had produced epic problems of police inefficiency in many cities. When middle-class and business interests began to feel threatened by these problems, a citizens' movement emerged that was embodied in the crime commissions that were set up in many cities.[56] The prototype was the Chicago Crime Commission, which was formed by the Chicago Association of Commerce when dissatisfaction reached a peak after the Winslow Brothers payroll robbery in the summer of 1917. The commission described itself as "a business proposition," not a "reform organization" or a "debating society."[57]

The Los Angeles Crime Commission was formed by business and insurance interests following a period of soaring property loss because of crime, so far out of control that the city had been threatened with loss of theft coverage by the insurance companies.[58] The city, which then had a population of 800,000, was run by political factions who were unresponsive to citizen demands for reform in policing, and illegal gambling houses flourished with the approval of city and police officials. As a result, the department faced a major problem of controlling police graft and incompetence.

Whatever Vollmer's expectations when he took the job, the Los Angeles experience reinforced his natural cynicism about the difficul-

[56] See Virgil Peterson, "The Crime Commission," *Conference on Criminal Law Enforcement*, Conference Series No. 7, University of Chicago Law School (March 2, 1951), 74-77.

[57] "The Chicago Crime Commission," editorial in the *Journal of the American Institute of Criminal Law and Criminology*, 10 (1919): 8-12.

[58] Deutsch, *op. cit.*, p. 140.

ties of working in a city with entrenched corruption. He first moved against the gambling houses, operating from information provided by undercover police groups that he had established himself. The raids were directed by officers personally selected by him for their honesty.

Vollmer's appointment to head the L.A.P.D. and his actions after assuming the job were front page news. He had an excellent national reputation, and to the people who sponsored his appointment he must have seemed like their last hope to bring adequate policing to the city. Business and professional groups were organized in his support, and he had important backing from the newspapers. One paper regularly carried boxed statements of Vollmer quotes that were titled, in bold lettering, "VOLLMER SAYS. . . ."[59]

But the connections between political figures and underworld interests were too tenacious to permit reform to take place. Public officials who supported him in the press worked to undercut him behind the scenes. In an undated, handwritten letter during this year to Millicent Gardner Fell, whom he married right after returning to Berkeley, Vollmer gave a glimpse into the extent of the corruption he faced.[60] A meeting was arranged for him with the "Kings of the underworld" by Walter Petersen, who was ousted as chief of the Oakland department after criticisms from religious and citizen groups who accused him of failing to enforce the vice laws.[61] Vollmer commented that he did not believe that his old friend and mentor was dishonest: "It was the old system to permit gamblers to operate up to the limit of what the people would allow, and in return the gamblers protected the town by keeping the thieves and bunco men from operating in the city that afforded them protection."

At the meeting Vollmer was introduced to a "well-known Oakland gambler," who told him that the underworld interests who had financed the mayor's campaign were upset by Vollmer's crackdown on gambling. In return for being more "liberal" in his enforcement, Vollmer would be promised the cooperation of the city government in other areas. If he did not cooperate, the mayor would be disgraced and "the hounds would immediately be unloosed." Vollmer did not give a negative answer at the time because he did not want to "lose

[59] Unidentified clippings in the Vollmer Collection.
[60] Vollmer Collection.
[61] See our discussion on pp. 101-102.

an interesting connection in the crooked chain." "Of course, you know what the answer will be, but before I say no, I'd really like to know a little more of the story."

Vollmer did not cooperate with the underworld and as a result was the target of continual harassment. At one point officials tried to force his resignation by requiring him to take a civil service examination for the position he already held, an open insult for a man of his standing; but he took the examination and received the highest score of those participating.

Vollmer's own actions during the year may be divided into two parts. Outside the department, he worked to consolidate public support for police reform by addressing citizen groups and social clubs which represented the progressive element in the city. He was instrumental in forming betterment associations in several areas, such as the L.A. Academy of Criminology and the L.A. Child Guidance Clinic. He was active in efforts to approve the building of a modern county jail and spoke out for penal reform.

Within the department, Vollmer introduced several technical reforms—beat analysis, improved traffic control, and *modus operandi* files—but concentrated upon upgrading the quality of personnel. He bypassed the city's strict civil service system by requiring all officers to take intelligence and psychological tests that, according to one account, discovered that many of the officers were "low-grade mental defectives" and that "three out of every four cops were unfit for police work."[62] Using the tests as the criterion, Vollmer promoted a number of capable junior officers and established stricter entrance requirements for future recruits.

Following the Berkeley model, Vollmer also initiated ties with the educational community. A police school was started within the department, and extension courses in police administration, designed for middle-management staff, were established at the University of Southern California.

The most tangible outcome of Vollmer's work in Los Angeles, however, was a detailed analysis of the department that included recommendations for increasing efficiency and raising personnel standards. This report was ignored after his departure but was revived in 1949 and used as a guide for restructuring the department.

The crime commission that had brought Vollmer to Los Angeles also engaged in the rewriting of outdated portions of the criminal

[62] Deutsch, *op. cit.*, p. 141.

code and sponsored changes in the state penal code. The city's newspapers were strongly in support of these measures, which, taken in combination with Vollmer's enforcement efforts, resulted in a significant decrease in the crime rate. However, the commission failed to realize how difficult it would be to maintain its successes; after its term expired, it considered its job done and ceased to operate. With this organized citizen pressure withdrawn, the old political factions quickly reestablished their control over city services.

Vollmer had bitter memories of his year in Los Angeles, perhaps capped by a highly publicized scandal in which a woman accused him of breach of promise and allegedly attempted suicide on his account. The case was nearing the court stage when Vollmer returned to Berkeley. He received letters of support and aid from friends in Los Angeles and conducted an aggressive investigation of the woman's underworld connections in support of a countersuit he had filed against her for defamation of character. The woman eventually dropped her charges before a trial could be held.[63]

"The best that I could do with Los Angeles was to present the city with a constructive program," Vollmer wrote to a supporter after he left.[64] Nine years later he wrote pessimistically of the outlook for reform in that city: "[I]t is my opinion that under the present system and laws the police department of Los Angeles can never be separated from politics, nor be free from the vicious and frequently unfounded attacks made upon the department by some of the newspapers and preachers of Los Angeles. . . . And from what I know of the people of Los Angeles, it is unlikely that they will make any radical change. . . ."

He believed that this situation existed not only in Los Angeles but "in all of our large cities." The core of the problem was vice law enforcement: "It is my opinion that it is absolutely impossible for any chief of police or any police department, however well it may be organized and equipped, to eliminate gambling, prostitution, and bootlegging in the city of Los Angeles."[65]

As part of this larger picture, Vollmer's term in Los Angeles was not successful, in that he was unable to implement basic reforms that survived his absence. But he was correct in aiming his efforts at improving personnel standards, and he left a cadre of committed

---

[63] See clippings and letters for the year 1924 in the Vollmer Collection.
[64] Letter dated Aug. 13, 1924, to Dr. Aaron J. Rosanoff, Vollmer Collection.
[65] Letter dated June 3, 1933, to Mr. Guy E. Marion, Vollmer Collection.

officers within the department who exerted influence over operations in later years when they assumed leadership positions. If Vollmer had stayed in Los Angeles, it is doubtful that even a man of his forceful personality could have prevailed against entrenched corruption in the way that he did in Berkeley. Without the community ties that validated and sustained his actions, Vollmer was merely a capable and honest administrator, not an influential citizen who could shepherd his ideas through the city forums.

One observer has noted that in Berkeley, Vollmer "pushed crime north and south."[66] He created an enclave of effective law enforcement, a haven from the urban centers that surrounded it. No such strategy was possible in a city of 800,000 that existed as the primary urban center for a very large region, especially in a city as disordered geographically as Los Angeles. Crime could not be pushed north or south; it could only be deferred or moved to another part of the city itself. It was inevitable that the most durable of Vollmer's innovations in Los Angeles were the techniques and procedures that could bring increased efficiency into a department that had to police a large, decentralized city. The other side of his concept of policing—the policeman as a "social worker," the commitment to community involvement—had very limited application in that setting.

Surveys and Research

Vollmer did not serve as police chief in any other city, but he conducted several important police surveys. In late 1926 he spent three months in Detroit, suggesting many improvements in police operations. He stirred up controversy at the conclusion of his study in a press interview by criticizing the Detroit judiciary, "characterizing one [judge] as a lazy psychopath and two as political favorites of the underworld. This criticism aroused considerable interest in the city."[67]

In 1928 he surveyed the Kansas City, Mo., police department and encountered the same kind of municipal corruption as in Los Angeles. Uncontrolled crime and ineffective city services had brought virtual chaos to the city, reflected in property insurance rates that were the highest in the country.[68] Vollmer recommended that the

[66] Interview with John D. Holstrom, *op. cit.*, p. 32.
[67] *National Municipal Review*, March 1927, p. 209.
[68] Deutsch, *op. cit.*, p. 143.

department be entirely removed from local control and placed under the authority of a state commission. This style of police control, known as metropolitan policing, had precedents in New York City in 1857 and Boston in 1885, in both instances following long-term struggles between state and city.[69] In Kansas City, reforms were attempted under the new structure but were short-lived; the state courts ruled that the commission was unconstitutional, and local political officials regained control.

These surveys were an important vehicle for introducing Vollmer's ideas about police reform into departments throughout the country. He was a sincere advocate and brought with him information about the latest procedural and equipment advances that were available. His survey methods were used by the I.A.C.P. and the International City Manager's Association as the basis for their series of textbooks in municipal administration.[70]

In 1928 Vollmer was hired by the Illinois Commission for Criminal Justice to do a report on the Chicago Police Department. This survey began a new phase in Vollmer's career, which resulted in his appointment to the faculty of the University of Chicago. There was considerable interest among influential Chicago citizens in the possibilities for reforming the police in that city, which was deeply scarred by the infiltration of organized crime; Chicago had one of the longest traditions of criminal involvement in government and policing of all American cities. Vollmer's recommendations followed the pattern of his earlier studies, but lacking a commitment for reform from the ruling political factions, few real changes resulted from his efforts.

One of the important people in the citizens committee was Julius Rosenwald, owner of the Chicago-based Sears, Roebuck Company.[71] He and Charles E. Merriam, a long-term political figure in Chicago and member of the political science department at the university, believed that the university should become involved in a "systematic and scientific effort to improve American police organization and methods." They recruited Vollmer to be part of a program that

[69] See James F. Richardson, *The New York Police: Colonial Times to 1901* (New York: Oxford University Press, 1970), pp. 96-99; and Roger Lane, *Policing the City: Boston 1822-1885* (Cambridge, Mass.: Harvard University Press, 1967), pp. 217-219.

[70] Interview with Milton Chernin, *August Vollmer: Pioneer in Police Professionalism, op. cit.*, p. 13.

[71] Material on this subject is largely taken from an unpublished interview with Spencer D. Parratt, 1973.

included Ernest W. Burgess, professor of sociology, in crime and parole; L. Thurstone in psychology; Raymond Moley in criminal justice; and Herman Adler, a psychiatrist working in juvenile delinquency. Vollmer was hired both to teach and conduct research. Merriam wrote to him: "We intend, if possible, to establish a great center for the scientific study of police work, with the whole country as our field of action." The program was to be based in academic research but still capable of making a direct impact on police methodology.[72]

This was Vollmer's most ambitious involvement so far with higher education. He taught courses in police administration with the assistance of Spencer Parratt, who had worked with Vollmer on police surveys and was at that time a graduate student at the university. Some of the students were young recruits with the Chicago Police Department, but the program was not designed merely to train police officers. Vollmer taught in Chicago for two years and during this time assisted in organizing the Regional Peace Officer's Association and the Illinois State Identification Bureau. He and Parratt also supervised a survey by students of police departments within a fifty-mile radius of Chicago.

Vollmer returned to Berkeley in 1931. According to Parratt, financial support for the program was withdrawn by the Rosenwald Fund, and it was not developed into the research center for police issues that its originators had planned. However, Vollmer was also having health problems that forced him to begin limiting his activities. He had difficulties with his eyes that required him to curtail his reading and to rest during the day, a regimen that seriously hampered his teaching and research. It is likely that Vollmer's return to Berkeley was occasioned by these problems as well as his and his wife's preference for the California city.

While in Chicago, Vollmer had been on leave of absence from the Berkeley Police Department. He resumed his position as chief when he returned, but in less than a year—in June of 1932—he retired at the age of fifty-six after twenty-seven years as marshal and chief of the Berkeley department. His correspondence reflected two different reasons for his retirement at this time. While still in Chicago, Vollmer was in touch with officials at the University of California concerning an appointment there and exchanged letters with City

[72] Letter dated May 1, 1928, in the Vollmer Collection.

Manager Hollis Thompson about the possibility of splitting his time between the university and the department or of quitting the department in favor of a full-time job at the university. However, after his resignation he wrote to friends that his action was precipitated by a dispute over police salaries. The Depression was forcing the city to cut back on salaries, and Vollmer told Thompson that he would quit if police officers were included in the cutback. The salaries were in fact lowered shortly thereafter, and Vollmer retired within a few months.[73]

[73] See letters for 1931-1932 in the Vollmer Collection.

4 THE NATIONAL SCENE

Crime is big business and requires police executives of unusual ability to prevent it from destroying governmental foundations.

Vollmer, *Report on Police* (1931), p. 26

WICKERSHAM REPORT

In 1931 the federal government added its voice to those of academics, police leaders, and citizen groups who were scrutinizing problems of crime and law enforcement. The Wickersham Report, produced by the National Commission on Law Observance and Enforcement, was the first attempt by the government to provide an overview of police problems, to suggest reforms, and to set standards.

The commission was set up by President Hoover to report on the status of law enforcement near the end of a decade in which Prohibition and social turmoil had demoralized and reduced the effectiveness of the nation's agencies of criminal justice. It was similar in scope to the 1967 President's Commission on Law Enforcement and the Administration of Justice, which also dealt with police problems after a period of social upheaval and resultant criticism of the criminal justice system.[1]

Hoover had promised to appoint such a commission when he received the Republican nomination in 1928, but it had been intended to examine more narrowly the workings of national Prohibition. After the election he set up the commission on the broadened mandate of pursuing "a searching investigation of the whole structure of our federal system of jurisprudence," in addition to looking at enforcement

[1] See *Task Force Report: The Police* (Washington, D.C.: U.S. Government Printing Office, 1967).

of the Eighteenth Amendment. The "wets" who favored repeal were disappointed at the change.[2]

August Vollmer was appointed to direct the police section of the Wickersham Report, which focused on police personnel and internal organization.[3] His two research assistants, David G. Monroe and Earle W. Garrett, who were attached to the Department of Political Science at the University of Chicago, did most of the research and actual writing of the report; Vollmer wrote the chapters on the police executive.

This appointment represented the high point of Vollmer's influence as a national police leader. The Wickersham Report articulated standards and goals in policing that have remained relatively unchallenged. It provided forthright documentation of the general low standards of policing and of the disaffection of the public with their police agencies. "[L]aw enforcement agencies," wrote Vollmer in the report, "are usually held in contempt, and law enforcement is one of our national jokes."[4] Most important for the development of professional policing, it established as first priorities the removal of politics from policing and the independence of the police function.

In outlining the qualifications necessary for the police executive, Vollmer centered upon the need to protect the chief from removal without cause. He noted the theory that a strong executive would produce an autocratic police department but asserted that "the people have gone too far in attempts to limit the control of police executives. . . .[T]heir attempt to protect themselves from a powerful autocratic chief of police has served to place them and the government in the hands of unscrupulous cutthroats, murderers, and bootleggers."[5]

Many chiefs at that time were swept in and out of office along with the political administrations of their city and had little chance to build a protective power base. Appointees were often merely party hacks with little or no experience in policing. Vollmer quoted an Indianapolis mayor who appointed his tailor to be chief: "He knows how to make good clothes; he ought to be a good chief." In contrast, the Milwaukee department had had only two police chiefs in forty-six

[2] Andrew Sinclair, *Prohibition: The Era of Excess* (Boston: Little, Brown, 1962), p. 361.

[3] *Report on Police* (Washington, D.C.: U.S. Government Printing Office, 1931).

[4] *Ibid.*, p. 17.

[5] *Ibid.*, pp. 50-51.

years, and politicians had been unable to establish control over internal police operations.[6]

But the record in most cities was bleak. In a consoling letter written in 1934 to an ousted St. Louis chief, Vollmer said: "New York with four police commissioners in four years and Detroit with four commissioners in one year give convincing proof that the people of America are suffering from the effects of an overdose of chloroform because their profound lethargy cannot be otherwise explained."[7] As a strong leader himself, Vollmer knew the value of leadership in an organization that had a paramilitary structure, and he felt that policing was demeaned by the appointment of "cronies" to jobs that required a skilled and dedicated officer.

The familiar recommendations that Vollmer listed at the conclusion of the study provided what he considered to be the baseline or minimum standards necessary for professional policing: removal from politics, independence of the chief, high recruitment and training standards, good working conditions, modern communications and records systems, and an active crime prevention unit. On the state level, he recommended state police organizations "where rural protection of this character is required" and advocated the establishment of bureaus of criminal investigation and information in every state.[8]

WORKING AT THE UNIVERSITY

The publication of the report coincided with Vollmer's return to Berkeley and, within a few months, his retirement from active police work. In the years that followed, he made it a point of etiquette not to visit Berkeley police headquarters without an invitation from the new chief, but he continued to exercise considerable influence over department affairs from his home on Euclid Avenue in the Berkeley hills.[9] Many of the officers that he had trained in the department in earlier years were now in important positions in other

[6] *Ibid.*, pp. 20-21, 43.

[7] Letter dated Jan. 9, 1934, to Col. Joseph A. Gerk, Vollmer Collection, Bancroft Library, University of California, Berkeley.

[8] *Op. cit.*, p. 140.

[9] Interview with John D. Holstrom, *August Vollmer: Pioneer in Police Professionalism* (interviews conducted by Jane Howard Robinson, Regional Oral History Office, Bancroft Library, University of California, Berkeley, 1972), p. 15.

cities, and Vollmer maintained a very active correspondence with them, exchanging ideas and advice and using his influence to help their careers.

Before he began his work as research professor at the University of California, Vollmer and his wife spent a year traveling through Europe and Asia. He developed contacts with many foreign police officials during this trip, especially in England. He visited Germany the week after Hitler was elected to power; after commenting favora-- bly in a letter about the selection and training techniques of the German police, he said: "Of course, any person with a grain of intelligence will recognize the fact that all of the training is not just for police purposes. The Germans are unquestionably utilizing this method to prepare men for war, and should they go to war in the immediate future they will not be unprepared."[10]

Vollmer's appointment to the university was the result of a Rockefeller Foundation grant for a project in the administration of criminal justice, conducted by the Bureau of Public Administration and the Department of Political Science. The project also brought psychiatrist Herman Adler from Illinois and recruited Hugh Fuller, an expert on criminal statistics. A new group major in criminology was being offered by 1933, and Vollmer taught courses in police administration in addition to his research.

The police curriculum that Vollmer and others designed at the university was intended to give the student a general education in academic subjects relevant to the field. It was not meant to be a technical police school within a university setting. Behind the program was Vollmer's dream of a minimum B.A. requirement for police recruits. If this were possible, he wrote in a letter to Bruce Smith, "do you not believe that the entire [police] service in America would be measurably improved?" He explained that the present program would "give to the prospective policeman rather a sound foundation in the tool and discipline courses and also require him to become acquainted with police practices and procedures in cities near the university." In the future the curriculum could add the more special- ized police courses, "but a very substantial beginning might be made with the facilities that are now offered at every university, providing that the courses were assembled and passed upon by people who

[10] Letter dated Sept. 1, 1933, to O. W. Wilson, Vollmer Collection.

have knowledge of the police problem and are sympathetically interested in promoting the welfare of police organizations."[11]

Vollmer solicited advice from Wilson and others about the existing courses they felt would be most valuable to a future policeman. Wilson prefaced his list by saying that "too great emphasis cannot be laid upon the importance of the first five subjects mentioned." They were public speaking, sociology, psychology, abnormal psychology, and statistics.[12]

Vollmer was realistic about the level of support he could expect from police chiefs in promoting a university education for policemen. After mentioning in the Smith letter that he planned to send a questionnaire to all American police chiefs to solicit their opinions on police education, he wrote: "Don't laugh. I know exactly what you are thinking after having read the foregoing, but don't forget that there are a few of my friends in the police service who are really interested in the police service, and I would not be surprised that we shall have, out of the 1,000 or more requests that we shall make, somewhere in the neighborhood of 15 or 20 responses. ... Perhaps 50 years from now, or possibly 100, we may have university-trained policemen."

Even his friends chided him for his worship of the "false god" of education and degrees. To an old friend and protégé he retorted: "[I]t will probably suffice to say that I never have worshipped false gods and have never bowed in abject subjection before those gaily decorated sovereigns that are sometimes termed degrees." He knew that a university education could not make the wrong kind of person into a good policeman, and he knew that some of the best officers had almost no formal education at all. "Just remember that we have had considerable experience with university men in our police department, and we have invited quite a number of them out for incompetency." But the university could draw together the subjects that would make the right kind of person into a very good policeman; and "every individual will come to respect the police service more when it is certain that every individual member has been specially trained for his job."[13]

Vollmer was fully realistic about the limitations of police education although he reserved the greater measure of his skepticism for

[11] Letter dated Sept. 11, 1933, Vollmer Collection.
[12] Letter dated Aug. 6, 1931, Vollmer Collection.
[13] Letter dated Sept. 26, 1933, to W. A. Wiltberger, Vollmer Collection.

private exchanges. He also assigned great importance to status, to
the greater respect that the policeman would receive when he had
more credentials on his side. Being a generalist, Vollmer's professional
policeman would have to acquire those credentials as an individual
rather than by participating in a professional organization—the police
department—that would give him technical schooling. That was why
Vollmer had to transcend the limits of the police academy in favor
of a university education. If he had envisioned the professional police
organization as a collection of specialized officers, each narrowly
trained to perform a technical skill, and if he had perceived the patrol
function to be more mechanical and limited in scope, there would
have been no need for a general university education. In his view,
only higher education could give true legitimacy to professional
policing.

The goal of having college-educated patrolmen on the streets
of many cities was, Vollmer admitted, a dream for the future. Of
more immediate importance to him, both in Chicago and at the
University of California, was his contact with talented students who
could be drawn into the cause of professional policing. He considered
his own role to be the training of leaders and the continuation of
lobbying efforts to set up police education programs in existing
colleges and universities.

California's present lead in police training, both in-service and
academic, is a direct result of the Vollmer influence. In 1930 he and
Earl Warren, then district attorney of Alameda County, combined
efforts to set up a police science training program. This began as
an extension course at San Jose Teachers College and soon evolved
into a two-year academic program in police science and administration. A former Berkeley police officer was recruited to head the
program, which included internship experience with the San Jose
Police Department. In 1935 this program became the San Jose State
College Police School. A similar program was established at Los
Angeles Junior College in 1934.[14]

"A MAN OF FADS AND FANCIES"

Vollmer was a nonconformist in his views on police education
but even more so in his opposition to some of the punitive practices

[14] John P. Kenney, *The California Police* (Springfield, Ill.: Chas. C Thomas, 1964), p. 99.

of American criminal justice. One of the characteristics of the "old" policing that Vollmer hoped to eliminate was the use of the third degree. The Wickersham volume *Lawlessness in Law Enforcement* had provided documentation of the routine use of brutality and intimidation by police against suspects.[15] When solicited in confidence by the commission for his views, Vollmer replied: "The use of the third degree is an admission of stupidity and ignorance and brutality."[16] Some police chiefs denounced the "lawlessness" volume of the Wickersham Report, either denying its facts or arguing in private that policemen could not solve crimes without the use of some police intimidation.

Vollmer stood virtually alone among police leaders in his open opposition to capital punishment. Even his closest associates disagreed with his views on deterrence and the humanitarian treatment of prisoners. In 1931 he testified before a California assembly judiciary committee in favor of repealing the death penalty. A Sacramento newspaper columnist wrote that Vollmer was a "theoretical policeman," a "man of fads and fancies, with his head in the air and his feet never on the ground. He is accepted as an authority on penology by other dreamers upon the same subject; but practical men with far more than his experience in detecting and punishing crime do not rate him very high."[17] The opinions of many policemen must have been equally negative.

Vollmer's views on other social issues were surprisingly liberal. He was evidently untouched by the wave of anticommunism that arose during the Depression. In a 1930 letter he referred to a Berkeley newspaper editor as having a "bolshevic phobia." "It is well to keep in mind the activities of the communists in this country and be prepared to meet emergencies, but so far as I am able to discover they have little opportunity of putting over their propaganda unless our own government falls down on the job." He cited unemployment, failure to deal with crime, and grafting officials as the greater threat.[18]

In 1934 an official of the Berkeley Y.M.C.A. sought Vollmer's advice about allowing communist discussion groups to use the facilities of the Y. Vollmer urged him not to violate the "open forum"

[15] *Report on Lawlessness in Law Enforcement* (Washington, D.C.: U.S. Government Printing Office, 1931).

[16] Letter dated Dec. 15, 1930, to Mr. S. R. Gainer, Vollmer Collection.

[17] *Sacramento Bee*, April 17, 1931.

[18] Letter dated Nov. 3, 1930, to Jack Greening, Vollmer Collection.

tradition of his organization although he would have to expect a lessening of financial support. "We should only limit discussion when revolution by force is advocated. All other discussion, in my opinion, is good for the country. If the communists have arguments that are sufficiently convincing, why shouldn't we listen to them?"

At the request of this official, Vollmer wrote a letter on the subject of free speech to the local commander of the American Legion. Attempts to regulate free speech had always resulted "disastrously," he claimed. "I would give every soap orator in the state a free soap box and a private parking situation for his soap box, and I would let him talk until he needed throat tablets. If we haven't sufficient arguments to prove our own principles of government, then we should sink. Our present practice is to make martyrs out of a lot of dumbbells."[19]

A San Francisco friend was worried because his neighbors said he was considered by the police department to be a communist. "What do you care if the police department has you listed as a communist?" Vollmer wrote to him.

It couldn't do you a particle of harm, and it may do you considerable good. They wouldn't give you the information even if you attempted to corroborate it. However, I am reasonably certain that whatever record they may have is not in their official files; it may be included in the private record of the so-called red squad. This is the system in most police departments in order to prevent the courts from obtaining information from their secret files .... You are probably familiar with the fact that there is a self-appointed group known as the vigilantes who are 100 percent plus red-blooded Americans who are ferreting out reds, pinks, and near pinks, and sometimes these hardened patriots step clear over into the white. This was true, as you recall, during the World War, when every person who had a German name was suspected of being pro-German and was reported to the secret service authorities. In my position as instructor in the Intelligence Department, I scanned the names of hundreds of my good friends who were workers in the cause of our government and who were listed as pro-Germans. One of them, incidentally, was the deceased past president emeritus of this institution, Benjamin Ide Wheeler.[20]

[19] Letter dated Aug. 28, 1934, to Harry L. Kingman; letter dated Sept. 22, 1934, to Mr. Ralph Pieroy, Vollmer Collection.

[20] Letter dated Aug. 27, 1934, to Dr. Ralph Arthur Reynolds, Vollmer Collection.

Vollmer's frequent criticisms of police practices and the favorable attention that he received from the press inevitably created a degree of resentment among other police officials. His relations with the San Francisco Police Department were especially strained, although they worked together effectively on a number of occasions. One San Francisco captain had said of Vollmer during his years as chief that "he might be interesting and effective in Berkeley, but he was so full of theories that he wouldn't know how to get a practical police job done."[21]

Vollmer aggravated the feud at a meeting in Sacramento in the mid-1930s when he described the San Francisco police as "morons." The meeting was concerned with problems of police selection, and Vollmer had been proposing higher entrance standards for policemen. Captain Charles Dullea of the San Francisco department had responded pointedly that it was a fine *theory*; Vollmer countered by saying that he wasn't interested in the standards in San Francisco because they were a "bunch of morons." The remark was uncharacteristic of Vollmer, who was generally careful to maintain amicable relations with his neighbors.

Dullea, who was a powerful official in the San Francisco department, remained hostile to Vollmer for years. "[N]ot only was Dullea very unhappy with Vollmer, but that meant he was unhappy with ... the Berkeley police force and unhappy with Berkeley. I've been told by one of his drivers that as a Captain and later the Chief of Police of San Francisco, if he could, he would attempt to detour Berkeley because Berkeley was one of those things he wanted to ignore."[22]

Vollmer took steps to end the feud in 1944 or 1945 when John Holstrom became Berkeley's chief at the comparatively young age of 35 and inherited the tense relationship with the San Francisco department. Seeing that Holstrom needed some assistance to "break in" to local police circles, Vollmer called Dullea and asked him to help the new chief. Dullea met and liked Holstrom and became an important sponsor for him in his career in California policing.

MEASURES FOR CENTRALIZED POLICING

Vollmer worked at the university until 1937. Most of his time

---

[21] Interview with John D. Holstrom, *op. cit.*, p. 12.
[22] *Ibid.*, p. 13.

was spent in research and graduate seminars. His principal writing endeavor, entitled *The Police and Modern Society*, was a volume written for the Bureau of Public Administration as part of a series on criminal justice.[23] Published in 1936, this book was Vollmer's most valuable contribution to the literature of policing; it presented his views on the police role and the organizational structure required to support it.

He divided his discussion into six areas. They were major crimes, wherein the policeman's role as a crime fighter was most clearly defined; vice control, his most unpopular task and an area in which legislative repression "has failed miserably in execution"; traffic, which Vollmer reluctantly admitted into the ambit of police functions; general service; crime prevention; and personnel.

In conjunction with a graduate student in his program, Alfred Parker, Vollmer co-authored a book in 1935 called *Crime and the State Police*.[24] "I am not particularly proud of this volume," he wrote, "because the press people wanted a popular volume, and we had to put it in the desired form."[25] The book was largely written by Parker although its conclusions represented Vollmer's own views as well.

State policing was a long-term interest for Vollmer and was consistent with his tendency to try to bypass local corruption by vesting control in a higher authority. He and others failed in efforts to have a state police force developed in California, both because of regional splits and labor opposition. During 1920-1921 he had been a member of an American Institute of Criminal Law committee that surveyed the movement to establish state and metropolitan police. As noted above, he recommended metropolitan policing in Kansas City and once offered that alternative as a means of cleaning up the Los Angeles department.

Vollmer believed that centralized policing at the state level—the elimination of local boundaries and overlapping jurisdictions—was a vastly more efficient way to deliver services than through the jumble of police agencies that existed. In *Crime and the State Police* he asserted that "the ideal to be sought is a single state police force and complete elimination of village, town, municipal, county, and all miscellaneous state police forces."[26] He was keenly aware of the

[23] (Montclair, N.J.: Patterson Smith, 1971, reprinted from 1936 ed.).
[24] (Berkeley: University of California Press, 1935).
[25] Letter dated Feb. 21, 1936, to Spencer D. Parratt, Vollmer Collection.
[26] *Op. cit.*, p. 208.

political obstacles that prevented anything approaching this ideal from being implemented, but he also did not see much merit in the principle that it was preferable to have local control over police organization. He thought that "each state should have but one police organization, and all municipal forces, sheriffs and constables should be discarded" in favor of a state "Minister of Justice." He cited the success of this type of organization in Italy and France, and to a degree in England.[27]

A more moderate position on centralized policing was articulated in the Wickersham Report, in a portion under Vollmer's direction but not written by him. It stated: "Home-rule principles have a broad basis in the traditions of our people, and this is probably a healthful sign." Police problems are mostly local and "lend themselves best to solution by the community authorities."[28]

However, for Vollmer and many others, endorsement of centralized policing did not extend to the national level. There had been discussion among members of the Wickersham commission about the desirability of a national police force. Vollmer wrote in a 1932 letter that the idea had not been pursued because "our Constitution is so constructed that an amendment would be necessary to create such a force," and it was unlikely that such an amendment would pass. Some members of the commission also felt that the principle of national policing was undesirable. Vollmer believed that it would be a "dangerous experiment," except for interstate crime problems where a clear jurisdiction existed.[29]

Another measure that Vollmer was advocating in these years was universal registration through the fingerprinting of all citizens. In 1934 he published an article that listed the advantages it would bring to law enforcement, ranging from controlling aliens and sex perverts to preventing bigamy and screening civil service applicants. "Communists, anarchists, may be followed from place to place and their activities noted," and "injured and unconscious persons may be identified."[30] He did not express reservations that such a tool could be misused for political purposes.

[27] Letter dated Nov. 17, 1933, to Mr. Leonard H. Nusbaum; letter dated June 3, 1933, to Mr. Guy E. Marion, Vollmer Collection.

[28] Report on Police, op. cit., p. 124.

[29] Letter dated Nov. 17, 1933, to Mr. Leonard H. Nusbaum, op. cit.

[30] Journal of the American Institute of Criminal Law and Criminology, 25 (1934): 650-652.

In a 1933 letter to a journalist he said: "What about national registration, if not of the entire population, at least, of aliens? What about the possibility of making a federal offense for habitual offenders to go from one state to another without a federal permit?" He also suggested the elimination of federal grand juries to speed the prosecution of criminals.[31] In another letter he said that he favored the registration of all citizens rather than of one group and noted that legislation directed against one class would probably be unconstitutional. The key target of registration was variously labeled "transients" or "migratory and professional criminals."[32]

In lieu of compulsory registration, a move arose during the 1930s for the voluntary fingerprinting of citizens. Perhaps the greatest successes of this drive were achieved in Berkeley. In 1936 the city government went on record in support of the fingerprinting campaign, and the newspaper carried a photograph of Vollmer fingerprinting Dr. Robert G. Sproul, the president of the University of California. The action followed a "six-year educational drive carried on by local service clubs to acquaint citizens with the value of this form of identification."[33] Vollmer pointed out in 1936 that universal registration had the "unqualified endorsement" of President Roosevelt, the Attorney General, the director of the F.B.I., and numerous official agencies and service organizations. "It should not be done by law but should be a voluntary contribution by every self-respecting and law-abiding citizen as evidence of his loyalty to his country. ..."[34] A 1941 source reported that the Berkeley Police Department had a file of 56,000 civilian fingerprints—more than any other agency except the F.B.I.[35]

LATER YEARS

In 1937 Vollmer retired from the university and spent his time studying, writing, conducting police surveys, and corresponding with associates and police officials about police problems. Former Berkeley

[31] Letter dated Sept. 8, 1933, to Mr. Thomas S. Rice, *Brooklyn Daily Eagle*, Vollmer Collection.

[32] Letter dated May 29, 1935, to Mr. H. G. Wilson, Vollmer Collection.

[33] *Christian Science Monitor*, May 14, 1936.

[34] Letter dated Feb. 18, 1936, to Mr. James H. Corley, Vollmer Collection.

[35] W.P.A. Writers Program, *Berkeley: The First 75 Years* (Berkeley, Ca.: The Gillick Press, 1941), p. 132.

officers who were working in other cities wrote regularly to Vollmer, soliciting his advice on problems they faced. Some of their inquiries were very specific: "In the last six months we have had two rape cases involving a six- and an eight-year-old girl. To date we have made no progress in clearing these cases. Could you supply us with some information which might be of some value to us?"[36] An associate in Honolulu wrote to ask about the effect of powder marks on a body. Vollmer replied with the information, and further advised: "Don't forget ... to establish the foundation for a good, rounded four-year training course for policemen at the university. ... If you don't establish the principles of acquiring professional standards for police service, you will have missed the greatest opportunity that was ever given to a man."[37]

O. W. Wilson was chief of the Wichita department until 1939. He and Vollmer maintained a detailed correspondence, and Wilson frequently used his letters to outline his own developing philosophy. Wilson came to believe that police administration should be narrowed, that it should be more efficiently and specifically directed than it was in the Vollmer model.

A close associate of Vollmer contrasted the two men: "Wilson had a concept of the police function as being a function which was definable and which could be isolated and perfected. Vollmer didn't have that. Vollmer had a feeling that the police department was part of a larger whole."[38] In Wichita, Wilson worked to streamline police administration, to sharpen and focus the resources of technique and personnel that were available.

Although he agreed with Vollmer about the importance of high standards in police training, he did not believe that the line officer needed the quality of education that Vollmer was aiming for in his quest for college-trained policemen. Writing to Vollmer about the Kansas Police School in 1939, Wilson said: "Training the subordinate officers is futile if commanding officers are unsympathetic toward new ideas and fail to take advantage of modern procedures. ... The return on the training effort would be much greater in the case of commanding officers."[39]

[36] Letter dated May 6, 1939, from O. W. Wilson, Vollmer Collection.
[37] Letter dated Aug. 30, 1935, to Mr. W. A. Gabrielson, Vollmer Collection.
[38] Unpublished interview with Spencer D. Parratt, 1973.
[39] Letter dated Jan. 16, 1939, Vollmer Collection.

Concerning crime prevention, Wilson asked Vollmer's "advice and counsel" on limiting police involvement to community activity, rather than to "adjustment work." Wilson quoted a statement from Millspaugh's work on crime prevention that asserted: "[C]rime prevention cannot under present circumstances be viewed as a logical or practicable police function. ...." Police work "must be sharply focused on the detection and apprehension of law breakers. Other specialized activities should be left to other and more appropriate agencies."[40] It was a view that was in direct contradiction to Vollmer's philosophy.

The Wichita department did a study of the effectiveness of *modus operandi* in identifying perpetrators of crimes or identifying a crime as one of a series. "We started the study in the honest belief that we would be able to prove the value of MO," but their conclusions seemed to prove the opposite. Wilson sent a copy of the study to Vollmer for his reactions. "[T]he fact that MO has not really been taken hold of by the American police may be accounted for by the conclusions reached."[41]

Wilson did not change his mind about the limitations of *modus operandi*. In *Police Administration* he wrote: "The technique is of less utility in the United States [than in Britain] because of the indiscriminate nature of street crimes, unpredictable youth-gang criminal patterns, and the prevalence of crime resulting from drug addiction."[42] Vollmer's greater enthusiasm for *modus operandi* was consistent with his tendency to emphasize the police role in examining criminality itself.

Vollmer's letters for this period also reflected his continuing interest in the development of the lie detector. He recognized that "as far as the courts are concerned, the results obtained thus far by the use of the instrument would not be admissable as evidence," but he hoped that scientific experimentation would eventually change that. He believed the instrument to be a "very important and valuable tool" for police departments in their job of "clearing suspects and detecting guilt."[43]

[40] Letter dated Feb. 28, 1938, Vollmer Collection. The Millspaugh book was published by the Brookings Institution, Washington, D.C., 1937.
[41] Letter dated March 19, 1939, Vollmer Collection.
[42] (New York: McGraw-Hill Book Co., 1972), p. 383.
[43] Letter dated Jan. 29, 1934, to Capt. R. A. Snook, Vollmer Collection.

He also approved the use of the lie detector to uncover police dishonesty. In Los Angeles he tested officers to find the one who had stolen a revolver. During his 1934 survey of the Santa Barbara Police Department, during which the newspapers headlined: "Police Look for Shakeup Result of Vollmer Trip," he had lie detector tests administered to all the officers in the city council chamber room. They were required to answer such questions as, "Did you ever ask for or receive a bribe?" and "Have you ever stolen anything since you have been in police work?"[44] In his letters to Keeler, who was working in Chicago, Vollmer offered practical suggestions for the improvement of the device and the appropriate circumstances for its use.

Vollmer was aware of the limitations of the lie detector, but as an advocate he was not inclined to be critical or skeptical about its possibilities. When he was still in Chicago, he had participated in an interesting experiment that was intended to verify or discredit the claims of prisoners at the Illinois State Penitentiary at Joliet that they were innocent of their crimes.[45] Keeler administered lie detector tests to a group of selected inmates, and their stories were checked against the court records from the trials. Herman Adler, a psychiatrist, was retained to interview each prisoner.

Although the project was never completed, the testing indicated that the prisoners were telling the "truth," even though their statements frequently differed substantially from the court records. Over the years that they had been in prison, they had developed accounts of their convictions in which they believed and which were registered as truthful by the instrument. In other words, the lie detector was useless in these circumstances in determining whether or not any of the prisoners were innocent.

For most of the time in these later years Vollmer stayed close to home. He conducted a seminar in his home on police surveys with two senior officers of the Berkeley department and encouraged several others in their various writing and teaching projects. Charles Gain, later chief of the Oakland department, met Vollmer during the early 1940s when he was a young patrolman and was so impressed by his personality and ideas that he returned several times for long discussions about policing.[46]

[44] The *Santa Barbara Morning Press*, April 21, 1934.

[45] Material on this subject is taken from an unpublished interview with Spencer D. Parratt, 1973.

[46] Personal interview, January 1972.

Vollmer persuaded the Charles C Thomas Publishing Company to begin a series on law enforcement, which accelerated the development of a technical literature for use in police departments.[47] He and Parker also wrote a book entitled *Crime, Crooks, and Cops,* of which he said: "[T]his is in a class with Heine Faust pot-boilers—only much worse!"[48] There was a considerable market in those days for popular works on crime and policing, but Vollmer's professional reputation was not enhanced by his willingness to participate in writing projects of this sort.

During the Second World War, Vollmer was active in a group called the Pacific Coast Committee on American Principles and Fair Play, of which Dr. Sproul was honorary chairman.[49] It was an organization of persons attempting to moderate the hostility against the Japanese-American community. The committee was generally in support of government policies but urged that relocation be a civilian not a military responsibility. It fought the efforts by some groups to pass legislation discriminatory against the Nisei, including efforts to remove their citizenship. Vollmer served on the advisory board of the committee during its short existence between 1941 and 1945.

In 1946 Vollmer was again involved in defending the right of the Berkeley Y.M.C.A. to allow radical discussion groups on its premises. He wrote in a letter to a Berkeley newspaper that the "public should feel indebted to these campus agencies, and to certain churches in the vicinity of the university, which have bravely and wisely shouldered an unwanted burden which others should have shared." One angry, unsigned reply cited Vollmer's "evident approval of communism" and asserted that "America is entirely too generous with Free Speech." The letter concluded: "I agree with J. Edgar Hoover. It is time to stand up and be counted."[50]

Vollmer's last major book, *The Criminal,* was published in 1949.[51] Rather than focusing on police administration, he tried in this work to deal with the theoretical issues surrounding criminality. *The Criminal* resulted from Vollmer's attempt to involve policing in the

[47] Interview with O. W. Wilson, *August Vollmer, Pioneer in Police Professionalism, op. cit.,* p. 14.

[48] (New York: Funk & Wagnalls, 1937), letter dated April 18, 1941, to "My Dear Friends," Vollmer Collection.

[49] See the materials in the Vollmer Collection under this heading.

[50] Unidentified 1946 clippings in the Vollmer Collection.

[51] (Brooklyn: The Foundation Press).

mystery of crime itself. The etiology of criminal behavior was, from his earliest years in police work, Vollmer's favorite preoccupation. By 1949 he had left behind him some of the more simplistic thinking that had marked the criminological theories of the pre-1920 era. He had become suspicious of the claims of any one theory to explain significant portions of the "vastly complex nature of crime and criminality."[52]

The book was a compendium of theories from various disciplines, divided into chapters called biological, physiological, psychological, sociopsychological, pathological, and law enforcement aspects of crime. "Few persons have any knowledge regarding the real causes of delinquency," Vollmer said, and concluded that considerable basic research was needed in the field. "Criminology will be on solid ground when it follows in the footsteps of medical science."[53] An individual's early years would often give evidence of future delinquency, and communities should identify and treat these children through special programs. Vollmer also pointed out the inferiority of the statistics that were available on crime and urged their improvement. "Reliable statistics are to the public and legislators what the compass is to the mariner."[54]

Vollmer never abandoned the hope that science could find practical answers to problems of crime causation. "Teaching and research ought to travel hand in hand in schools of criminology."[55]

In 1951 Vollmer succeeded in seeing a school of criminology established on the Berkeley campus, the end result of his years of work to bring police education into the university. O. W. Wilson was appointed the first dean of the new school. Vollmer hoped that an academic criminology program would serve as a laboratory for new ideas and a sophisticated training ground for police leaders.

In the early 1950s, Vollmer was afflicted with Parkinson's disease, which interfered seriously with his ability to function without assistance. He then became aware that he had cancer as well and confided to several close friends that "he would never become a bed patient, a person who would be helpless and a concern to other people."[56]

[52] *Ibid.*, p. 19.
[53] *Ibid.*, p. 408.
[54] *Ibid.*, p. 420.
[55] *Ibid.*, p. 436.
[56] Interview with John D. Holstrom, *op. cit.*, p. 39.

He was also uneasy about the effects upon his mind of the medication he was required to take.[57]

In accordance with these strong feelings, Vollmer committed suicide with his service revolver, ending his life in 1955 at the age of 79. Although he had been married twice (his second wife, Pat, dying in 1946), Vollmer left no children.

Vollmer's ideals and personality had an immeasurable impact upon the lives of those who worked with him. He had a profound influence on the ambitions of several generations of Berkeley policemen who became police leaders on their own. In a field in which leadership abilities are traditionally preeminent, Vollmer was the outstanding leader of the first half of this century, and his own skills were inextricably related to the image of policing that he created.

[57] Unpublished interview with Austin McCormick, 1972.

5 VOLLMER'S NEW POLICEMAN

When we have reached a point where the best people in society
are selected for police service, there will be little confusion
regarding the duties of the members.

Vollmer, "Aims and Ideals
of the Police" (1922)

"Truly Exceptional Men"

Vollmer did not construct a formal definition of what he meant by
"professionalism" perhaps because for him it signified a person more
than a concept. The individual professional policeman is the most
prominent feature in Vollmer's ideas about policing, and all other
aspects of the model are contingent upon him.

What are the characteristics of this professional? He can be
described as an honest and educated officer who uses modern technology to increase his efficiency in meeting his primary responsibility,
the suppression of serious criminal activity. He has a detailed knowledge of his beat or area of assignment, and he understands the
multiple requirements of evidence collection. He is detached from
local politics and is able to deal equally with all social and economic
classes, gaining their respect and cooperation without recourse to
personal identification with any particular class.

Professionalism thus leads to a search for the "perfect man"
rather than toward any rigorous examination of the content and
social context of policing. Vollmer believed that "society needs and
must somehow obtain truly exceptional men to discharge police
duties." They must be of "superior intellectual endowment, physically
sound, and free from mental and nervous disorders; they must have
character traits which will insure integrity, honesty, and efficiency;
their personality must command the respect and liking of their
associates and of the general public." He contrasted these men with

officers having low intelligence and working within low morale departments who "join the ranks of the work-dodgers and become members of the useless, parasitical group of municipal ornaments."[1]

He recognized that some aspects of police work were more amenable to professionalization than others, but he resolved conflicts in function by relying upon the high abilities of the policeman who would confront them. In other words, he viewed the policeman as a *total entity* who was responsible for a wide range of tasks that had little inner consistency. With the significant exception of vice law enforcement, Vollmer was jealously protective in keeping these functions in the police jurisdiction, and he opposed the idea that certain tasks should be transferred to other agencies. (Although he was not happy with many of the trivial aspects of traffic and parking control, Vollmer accepted the traffic function itself as a legitimate and important police responsibility.)

In discussing the movement to establish "citizen's police" for patrol duties, he wrote: "[T]here is no substitute for policemen in the performance of the great number and variety of duties required of the protective and law enforcing arm of government."[2] In Berkeley, Vollmer was proud that during his years as chief there had been a substantial decline in private policing. In 1918, fewer than five security guards were employed in the city, including the industrial and warehouse districts.[3] He considered it appropriate that the regular municipal police should assume total responsibility for watchman functions.

In short, Vollmer's new policeman did everything. He solved complicated crimes through his skills in scientific detection; he performed the numerous lesser functions of community public safety; he enforced the law fairly and efficiently; and he maintained a constant communication with the people who lived and worked on his beat. Those impediments that stood in his way were usually the fault of inexperienced lawmakers or an uncooperative public.

What were the specific elements of the job that the new policeman was expected to do? In *The Police and Modern Society*, Vollmer

[1] *The Police and Modern Society* (Montclair, N.J.: Patterson Smith, 1971, reprinted from 1936 ed.), pp. 222-223.

[2] *Ibid.*, p. 216.

[3] Editorial entitled "A Progressive Police System in Berkeley, California," *Journal of the American Institute of Criminal Law and Criminology*, 9 (1918): 320.

dealt separately with the often conflicting functions of policing, extending from crime suppression to traffic control. With this work as a reference point, we will look in some detail at the professional policeman's sphere of operation. Deferred to the next chapter is discussion of the responsibility for enforcement of vice laws, which Vollmer regarded as an illegitimate aspect of police work.

SUPPRESSING MAJOR CRIME

The "enemy" is the criminal. Against this alien element in the community, the professional policeman is best equipped to wage battle. A look at any of Vollmer's works shows that he approached crime solving with the enthusiasm of a detective story fan. James Q. Wilson wrote of this enthusiasm: "The practical police officer's love of anecdote weakened his account of criminal patterns. His chapter on 'Major Crimes' emphasizes the bizarre, the professional, and the psychotic to the neglect of the commonplace."[4] But for Vollmer it was in confronting major crimes that the professional seemed most confident and alert, most able to exercise the skills of his true calling. Vollmer used case histories to illustrate measures that he favored adopting to assist the police in crime fighting, some of which he was able to introduce into the Berkeley department. The scientific crime laboratory, motorized policing, and sophisticated communications devices are examples.

State bureaus of identification were designed primarily to assist the policeman in his prime function of crime fighting. Vollmer frequently described a criminal case of homicide or robbery that stretched across several states and did not fail to point out that centralized files, accessible to all the jurisdictions involved, would have assisted in apprehending the criminal much earlier. One such case involved a man who married over a dozen women and murdered many of them. Vollmer commented: "The assistance that a system of checking the movements of persons traveling from one state to another would give to the police in their attempts to solve homicides and apprehend murderers must be obvious."[5]

In advocating these measures, Vollmer did not express any cautions about potential misuse for political purposes. In his view,

[4] Introduction to *The Police and Modern Society, op. cit.*, p. x.
[5] *Ibid.*, p. 24.

the truly professional policeman would not be construed as a political agent. What possible objection could law-abiding citizens have to measures that would permit the police to fight everybody's enemy—the criminal?

Faced with this heavy responsibility, the professional policeman could not exercise his skills if bound by local restrictions or denied information and assistance. Because "antiquated, localized, unpopular police departments are pitted against criminals, up-to-date in technique, equipment, and transportation facilities," the first remedy is a state police. "But this is not enough. The modern criminal no longer restricts his operations to one state, nor does he so often work alone. Today, crime is organized." A federal police force is needed for interstate law enforcement. Finally, the policeman on the beat should receive training "comparable to that of a lawyer or a physician."[6]

The solution of crimes like homicide, kidnapping, robbery, and burglary requires skills that far surpass those of the average citizen. A professional policeman is expected to view any unusual occurrence with a higher degree of sophistication and detachment than the untrained citizen; what appears to be a routine death must be treated as a potential homicide or suicide, and the officer must use modern methods of crime detection and data analysis to evaluate the evidence he collects. Beyond this, he must be aware of the legal requirements surrounding his investigation so that he does not jeopardize possible prosecutions.

The fact that a professional crime fighter would be called upon to exercise his skills to a greater degree in a poor or a minority community than in middle-class and wealthy ones was not seen as a fundamental problem. What American would not come to respect a skilled professional? He discussed the higher incidence of property crime and resistance to police investigations in poor neighborhoods: "Since the police are established for the protection of property as well as of persons, it follows, naturally, that they should be placed at the head of the list of enemies."[7]

For Vollmer, the inherent antagonism that these groups felt toward policemen simply reinforced the need for the policeman to be detached from community identification. He believed that the

[6] *Ibid.*, p. 8.
[7] *Ibid.*, p. 69.

demonstration of professional expertise was the surest way to gain the respect of these alienated segments of the community. He was opposed to residence requirements. "What mystic qualities do the hometown boys possess that are not found in others?" He blamed the idea on "unprincipled politicians" who were "getting votes for themselves or their party."[8]

Motorized policing, which met some resistance when Vollmer first introduced it into Berkeley, served to separate the policeman from the local community mechanically. In his lifetime Vollmer witnessed the overwhelming impact that the automobile came to make upon American culture and how it changed both crime and policing. He constantly stressed the new mobility of criminals and the inability of a locally based constabulary to maintain knowledge of their whereabouts.

In mobilizing the policeman to fight major crime, and in advocating that he be a part of a state police system, Vollmer did not believe that he was interfering with his ability to perform other functions as well. He never drew a distinction in organizational terms between crime patrol and local contact, between the "punitive" and the "preventive." In Berkeley, it is likely that some of these problems were resolved through the smallness of the scale or were worked out in the weekly meetings that influenced day-to-day police operations.

In arguing for the greater use of science and modern organization in the fight against crime, Vollmer was always aware that, despite the skills of the professional, crime control would remain an elusive and multifaceted problem. "As a practical policeman considering this survey of a crime situation, the author has no idle dreams of any facile, immediate solutions of its serious problems. Experience has indicated certain possibilities. . . ."[9] The police were unjustly blamed for the failure to solve spectacular crimes; he cited the 1928 murder of New York gambler Arnold Rothstein, when "newspaper publishers and the public characteristically disposed of the matter to their satisfaction by bringing about the dismissal of the Commissioner of Police."[10] Vollmer worked tirelessly to perfect the policeman's crime-fighting skills, then turned the dilemma back upon itself by looking

[8] Letter dated Sept. 9, 1939, to "Jack," Vollmer Collection, Bancroft Library, University of California, Berkeley.

[9] *The Police and Modern Society, op. cit.*, p. 16.

[10] *Ibid.*, p. 21.

at a field with "tremendous import," crime prevention. He hoped
that the police could become the vanguard for a war against "crime
and the criminal" that would be waged from a wholly new perspective.
It was the professional's ultimate role.[11]

TRAFFIC CONTROL

Vollmer recognized that a major effect of traffic law enforcement
was the loss of the public good will that is "so vitally essential to
the maintenance of law and order. . . ."[12] The proliferation of automobiles on the nation's streets had been met by local government with
such a multitude of regulations that "few indeed are the persons
who can travel the streets or highways without violating one or many
of them every hour of the day." Added to this problem was the poor
level of police personnel assigned to enforcement: "[S]ome of these
men, long used to dealing with criminals and unaccustomed to dealing
with normal citizens, treated traffic violators as if they were professional lawbreakers." This rudeness, "especially if shown to women
and accidental violators," brought ill will to the police department.[13]

The challenge of constructing national traffic codes and of
training both policemen and drivers to understand and adhere to
them was an obvious area for the development of professional
expertise. By the 1930s, Americans had become aware that there were
no easy answers to problems of traffic safety. (In 1932, there were
29,451 traffic deaths.)[14] Much of Vollmer's treatment of the subject
was devoted to various research results that had been produced in
the effort to identify factors of road conditions, vehicles, and driver
patterns that contributed to traffic safety. He stressed the need for
reliance upon "competent engineers" who could advise local communities and legislators about the feasibility of their traffic regulations.
He urged the establishment of driving schools for young people, plus
continuous programs of traffic education and community support
for the police in their job of traffic enforcement.[15]

On the question of parking enforcement, Vollmer was impatient
for several reasons. "No intelligent policeman can conceive it to be

[11] *Ibid.*, pp. 235-237.
[12] *Ibid.*, p. 119.
[13] *Ibid.*, pp. 144-146.
[14] *Ibid.*, p. 120.
[15] *Ibid.*, pp. 127-128.

a duty of his office to tag cars for overtime parking. It is a child's work and consumes time that should be employed profitably otherwise." It also led to "every form of destructive criticism." In many cities, efforts by citizens to have politicians "square the tag" led to further demoralization of police efforts.[16]

Vollmer remarked wistfully that if people would only "use ordinary intelligence and exhibit good manners when they are in automobiles," so many regulations would be unnecessary.[17] Because he was always opposed to the tendency to "overlegislate" social behavior, Vollmer was naturally disturbed by the quantity of rules and regulations, many mere confirmations of common sense, that had been entered on the books. "I may say to you that I am unalterably opposed to the attempt of the American people to regulate every phase of our conduct by law."[18]

GENERAL COMMUNITY SERVICE

As a practicing policeman, Vollmer had a keen understanding of the sometimes tedious tasks that consumed much of the policeman's day. "Ordinarily the public thinks of the police as 'thief catchers,' or more recently—especially the younger generations—as 'traffic cops.' Few know them as the useful and versatile servants that they actually are." This category of activity ranges from enforcement of lesser criminal laws to the handling of an "unusually large number of reports received by the police [which] concern matters that are entirely out of their sphere."[19]

Vollmer listed them as the following: enforcement of federal, state, and local laws that are not classified as major crimes; missing person searches; lost animal and property searches; disposition of dead bodies and investigations of suicides; handling the insane and feebleminded; riots as a result of strikes, subversive activities, and racial disagreements; inspection of businesses and health conditions; and miscellaneous public complaints.[20]

He stressed the need for police officers to be intelligently trained

[16] *Ibid.*, pp. 132-133.

[17] *Ibid.*, p. 134.

[18] Letter dated March 19, 1936, to Mr. Burton W. Marsh, Vollmer Collection.

[19] *The Police and Modern Society, op. cit.*, pp. 185-186.

[20] *Ibid.*, p. 149.

to handle the emotionally disturbed, to collect accurate information concerning suicides and other deaths, and to prevent domestic or neighborhood conflicts from erupting into feuding and violence. Added to this is the officer's general role as watchman. These miscellaneous and routine duties Vollmer labeled the "fundamental requirements of police work." They exist, little altered, from city to city. The basic police patrol—"designed to make it difficult for criminals to operate without detection and detention"—is seen as a formidable deterrent against criminal activity by the "community's weaker members." During patrol, the officer is also acting as the "eyes and ears of the police executive." He must be familiar with the people on his beat. Vollmer described this duty in terms reminiscent of the job of the old political functionary: "The rules require that the policeman make inquiries concerning the character, occupation, and habits of every resident of his beat so that whenever his superiors desire information about any person living within the area that he patrols, he can supply it without delay."[21]

Many of the service duties that fall outside of patrol, that is, those called into the department, become part of police work because "no other agency is equipped to give general service. . . . Tragedies as well as comedies fill the miscellaneous public files. . . ."[22]

One of the most controversial police functions in Vollmer's time was the response to strikes and riots. No other task "contains so many complex problems" as do these occurrences. "Few persons appreciate the necessity that the police maintain at least a skeleton organization sufficiently well trained and equipped to meet any emergency, disaster, or catastrophe which may occur."[23] Vollmer was strongly opposed to the use of national guard troops to quell disturbances, charging that their presence usually increased instead of ending the violence. "Inexperienced men often shoot or club upon the slightest provocation. . . ." Training in the "art of war" ill equips them for police duties. Restraint in the use of firearms is the prime tactic for avoiding bloodshed in riot situations. Vollmer described a riot by 6,000 unemployed persons in Minneapolis that lasted over three hours. "As it was, instead of using firearms the police used fists and clubs; no deaths resulted."[24]

[21] *Ibid.*, p. 217.
[22] *Ibid.*, p. 185.
[23] *Ibid.*, pp. 149-150.
[24] *Ibid.*, pp. 180-184.

Throughout the discussion of riots, Vollmer always pictured the police as being "in the middle"; after strikes were over, he charged, both sides accused the police of favoring the other. He did not feel, however, that the use of police in riots and strikes would jeopardize their image as neutral professionals in future contacts with the communities involved. It is likely that these functions, not creating the internal demoralization that vice law enforcement did, seemed to interfere less with the policeman's neutrality as a crime fighter, even though their effects on the community were similarly coercive.

CHANGING TIMES

Vollmer was ahead of many of his contemporaries in his perception that the police would have to work increasingly with all classes in society, not merely the working and lower classes. Rapid urbanization and the advent of the automobile were key factors in this change, and Vollmer was aware that the police would be operating at a higher level of visibility. The use of third-degree techniques and the routine violation of due process may be tolerated when applied almost exclusively against minorities, the poor, and recent immigrants; but these tactics are not tolerated when applied against the middle and upper classes or against the children of these classes. Policemen who followed only the traditional, expediential methods of order maintenance would be poorly prepared to function in this new atmosphere.

Vollmer was also correct in perceiving that the automobile and other technological aids had escalated the level of sophistication in crime and that the police had to possess the same aids if they were not to be left behind. He saw that the new mobility of criminals prevented the police from treating crime as a local phenomenon which they could control by knowing the population of their own and surrounding jurisdictions. Efforts to centralize law enforcement were logical responses to these changes.

The United States in the 1920s and 1930s was undergoing many confusing shifts that threatened to limit the ability of the policeman to exercise his skills in a stable environment. But there also seemed to be new areas of expertise that would help the policeman to manipulate rather than be manipulated by these shifts. Vollmer's lifelong efforts for crime prevention through work with the young are an indication of his faith in this new expertise. His attempts to link police efforts with those of other social agencies made him a part of the progressive social movement that was effecting reforms in many aspects of American life. Much of his renown with the social and legal scholars of the day came from his enthusiastic endorsement of new social science techniques in matters of police personnel, juvenile handling, and the treatment of offenders. He was allied with groups which were traditionally critical of the overextension of police power.

Contacts within Berkeley's academic community provided Vollmer with new ideas about improving police standards at a time when the police were becoming a more visible target for criticism. The introduction of intelligence and psychological testing into the Berkeley department provided one example of this. He was part of the movement to reinterpret crime as a symptom of a deeper social malaise and to alter the skills that would be needed to combat it. His good credentials as a progressive reformer gave added weight to aspects of his professional model that may be seen, from today's perspective, to have been more rigidly determined by the particular concerns of the day.

CRIME FIGHTER VERSUS SOCIAL WORKER

Although it is possible to trace an evolution in Vollmer's thinking in relation to crime causation and the work of the police, his basic approach was fixed as early as 1919—the movement toward a detached, centralized, humanitarian police force operating under strong personal leadership.

The value that he placed on community involvement, however, came inevitably into conflict with the professional's detachment from local political processes. A policeman who is a detached crime fighter has difficulty in maintaining the level of local community involvement that Vollmer outlined for him. He becomes, at best, an outside expert in his relations with different community groups; at worst, if he is poorly recruited and led, he becomes an alien agent of the state's coercive power.

Silver, in writing of how the police role changes during periods of concern over social disorder, commented: "Police forces come to be seen as they were in the time of their creation—as a sophisticated and convenient form of garrison force against an internal enemy."[25]

[25] Allan Silver, "The Demand for Order in Civil Society," in *The Police: Six Sociological Essays*, ed. David J. Bordua (New York: John Wiley, 1967), p. 22.

Under these circumstances, professionalism resembles increasingly the military model that Vollmer saw as inappropriate for police work. But he failed to perceive the extent to which his view of the policeman as a crime fighter would inevitably involve that policeman in the military analogy. The professional's detached status limits his contacts with groups to the extent that he becomes unaccustomed to the give-and-take of local political and social change.

Vollmer believed that the professional *must* remain detached to prevent seizure of police power by partisan interests. Underlying this conviction was the implied one that social conflict cannot be resolved or contained without the existence of a strong police presence, that friction among groups will destroy the social order if a detached police force does not curb the tendency toward anarchy. "Whatever else may be said of the American police, this fact should be more widely known; namely, that without the police and the police organizations, with all their many defects, anarchy would be rife in this country. ... The American police are justified, if for no other reason than because in their hands rests in large measure the preservation of the nation."[26]

Therefore, we can see that Vollmer's reforms were based on two beliefs which came to achieve primacy in his model of policing. First was the belief that social conflict among groups cannot be resolved without positive police presence, at least in a mediating capacity. His philosophy contained but did not credit the historical view that the police are involved in imposing majority values upon subgroups through the use of coercion and selective enforcement of the laws. In a contemporary setting, Skolnick has written of minority groups coming "to regard the police as a hostile army of occupation enforcing the status quo."[27] Vollmer believed that the police could maintain social and cultural neutrality while keeping the peace through the exercise of the professional skills.

Second, Vollmer believed that the crime fighting function had to determine the basic organizational structure of the police department, from recruitment through deployment of patrol resources. All other functions would be served within this framework; all management decisions would be made compatible with this goal.

Conflicts inevitably arose between these beliefs and Vollmer's

[26] *The Police and Modern Society, op. cit.,* p. 185.

[27] See *The Politics of Protest* by Jerome Skolnick (New York: Ballantine Books, 1969), pp. 268-269.

repeated insistence that the professional policeman should maintain a benevolent involvement in the community. His commitment to a centralized state police force was the logical outcome of the concept of the crime fighting professional. After he had reached this point, the vision of a well-rounded policeman who gained respect and cooperation through his judicious enforcement of the law and through efforts to assist people in their contacts with government was irretrievably lost. How would Vollmer or Berkeley citizens have reacted if the department had been superseded in its personnel and operations policies by a state police agency based in Sacramento?

As we have seen, Vollmer expected to resolve conflicts in police function by recruiting exceptional individuals into the police service and training them in the use of a wide variety of sophisticated techniques. The Berkeley Police School became an early model for other professional training programs around the country. Police professionalism, in his view, could master the new knowledge that was being developed in technology, in management, and in the behavioral sciences and could apply it toward solving police problems.

Vollmer's belief in education led him to two conclusions: that the professional policeman would be distinguished from his predecessors by the level of his formal training both before and after recruitment; and that new ideas from the universities could provide valuable insights into the causes of crime and the means for preventing it. ("[T]he university is indispensible. There are literally thousands of police problems that need to be studied! Police treatises on every conceivable subject need to be written! New police techniques require development—and so on ad [in]finitum!")[28] He was influenced in reaching both conclusions by his contacts with faculty members at the University of California.

Education imparted both dignity and independence to the professional policeman. It gave him the means to be an efficient crime fighter and elevated his occupation beyond the reach of partisan political interference. This belief by Vollmer that education could liberate the policeman, could raise him to a more secure position in the social order, was rooted as much in his own temperament as in any objective evidence he saw for the need to improve police training. A former colleague of Vollmer's when he was a research professor at the University of California during the 1930s has suggested that Vollmer's own lack of formal education led him to overesti-

[28] Letter dated Sept. 9, 1939, to "Jack," Vollmer Collection.

mate the benefits that social science, particularly psychiatry, could give to policing:

> During all his life, he read avidly and studied avidly in this area of personality development, including an attempt to find out what the biological, sociological, psychological, anthropological components of personality analysis and development were. . . . I had the feeling often times that he was beyond his depth in this kind of study . . . and that he often turned for guidance and counseling in these areas to men who might not have been the best minds in that particular area but whose advice and counsel he took perhaps with more trust than was justified.[29]

In constructing a crime fighter who would also be a crime preventer, Vollmer was equating the reliability of the policeman's technical aids with the assistance that he could expect from theories of crime causation. His most enduring legacy to policing has been his understanding of police administration and of the efficient use of police resources. His larger understanding of the policeman as a professional who is competent to deal with social problems has failed, in part, because he expected too much from education and, correspondingly, from the policeman who would acquire it. The centralized police model is a direct descendant of Vollmer's practical innovations in police management, manpower allocation, scientific detection, and criminal identification. Further levels of competence in this professional model—the policeman as a crime preventer, as a benevolent protector of the community, as a respected and believable agent of the state—fall down at the point where they depend upon the policeman's ability to overcome his orientation as a crime fighter and even as a member of a particular cultural group or class; in other words, they expect him to bridge the conflicts in his role through his own superiority as a person.

In describing the future professional policeman as "the cream of the nation," Vollmer was expressing a hope that policing would become the kind of service that would attract large numbers of superior individuals. But this was a risky basis upon which to formulate a practical program of police reform. The limitations in Vollmer's model of professionalism have become apparent as it has been applied in ordinary settings with the normal proportions of ordinary officers and police leaders.

[29] Interview with Milton Chernin, *August Vollmer: Pioneer in Police Professionalism, op. cit.*, pp. 5-6.

When Vollmer abstracted a new model of professionalism from his Berkeley experiences and his studies, many of its most successful features were minimized or omitted. It was obvious to him that the Berkeley style could not be duplicated in a hostile or unstable political atmosphere. Problems of size alone jeopardized its application in cities like New York, Chicago, and Los Angeles. But it is unlikely that he appreciated the extent to which his success in Berkeley depended upon the personalized policing that he constructed there, possibly because he was too close to its workings; it was difficult to weigh these intangible factors in the same scale as flashing alarm systems and automobile patrols.

Although throughout his career he wrote about the primacy of crime prevention, Vollmer's recommendations for centralized policing and technical aids in crime fighting came to overshadow it on a practical level. He could transfer to Los Angeles or Detroit a modern system of record keeping, intelligence testing, or squad car deployment, but he could not transfer the public support that Berkeley gave him, nor the scale of its problems, nor the basic stability of its political processes.

In his writings on professionalism Vollmer was unable to resolve this contradiction between the policeman as a crime fighter and as a credible local functionary. He effected a limited resolution in Berkeley through his own leadership, but the scheme that he constructed for application in other cities was never successfully put to a test.

6 THE EVILS OF VICE AND POLITICS

> There is scarcely a city in the United States in which the police department has not been used as the ladder by which political organizations have crawled to power.
>
> Fosdick, *American Police Systems* (1920), p. 115

Traditional American policing had been so deeply entangled in scandal and partisanship that Vollmer and other reformers despaired of improving the police while they remained within the political setting. At the core of the "sordid story," as Fosdick characterized it, was the problem of vice laws.

The enforcement of laws against gambling, liquor, prostitution, and drugs had become the police chief's most bitter responsibility. If he enforced the law strictly, he was likely to suffer retaliation from the powerful interests which profited from illegal vice operations and to alienate those people in the community who were served by the operations. If he did not, he was open to virulent attack from civic and religious groups which believed open vice to be the worst problem of city life.

Underlying this controversy was a clash between traditional rural American values and the new dominance of urban centers. Skolnick has argued that the zeal of the moral reformers was as rational as the self-interest and concern with property crime that motivated the civic reformers. Prohibitionists were involved in a "test of strength between conceptions of social order: on the one side, the social order associated with the villages, and farms, and sectarian and fundamentalist Christianity; on the other side, the threat posed by the ever-increasing social influence and style of life of the cities, of industrialization, of a Romanized and Anglicized Christianity, and of immigration."[1]

It was a clash that placed the police in a particularly ambiguous position. In these pages we will look at some of the public attitudes that influenced Vollmer and his colleagues in their ideas about professional policing. Vollmer's own approach, the degree of change that he recommended, was often at odds with the views of his contemporaries; but the direction of the reform was unmistakable.

VICE LAWS: EXTREMISTS AND SKEPTICS

Any philosophy of policing operates best under a system of rational laws that are endorsed by a consensus of the population. Difficult as this may be to obtain in any area of the law, where vice is concerned these criteria are endemically absent. It is not surprising that Vollmer considered vice law enforcement to be the most disagreeable part of police work. He and many other police leaders were pragmatic in their understanding of the futility of using police coercion to affect people's personal behavior and considered vice to be a social problem requiring educative answers not legal ones.

Illegal vice operations were front page news during Vollmer's career. When *The Police and Modern Society* was published in 1937, the story in the *San Francisco Chronicle* centered upon his comments on prostitution, headlining: "Legalization Only Hope—Vollmer."[2] A department's policies on vice law enforcement were its most visible area of activity, thanks to the vigilance of moral reformers. It was also true, during the 1920s and 1930s, that many policemen were in partnership with the racketeers to profit from the vice trade.

Part of the hysteria about vice operations stemmed from widely held notions that drunkenness, drugs, and prostitution were largely the refuge of "mental defectives" who contaminated society with the hereditary taint of feeblemindedness.[3] Prostitutes were also blamed

[1] "Morality and Social Dominance," in *Society and the Legal Order*, eds. Richard D. Schwartz and Jerome H. Skolnick (New York: Basic Books, 1970), pp. 85-86.

[2] March 21, 1937.

[3] See Mark Haller, *Eugenics* (New Brunswick: Rutgers University Press, 1963), pp. 103-104.

for spreading most of the venereal disease that existed and which, in the days before penicillin, was an even greater health problem than it is today.

For Vollmer, the root cause of the controversy was the public's "faithful and reverential devotion to the idea that the [vice] problem can be solved with the passing of repressive laws." His writings portray the zealous moral reformer as almost as great an enemy to society and policing as the hardened criminal. "Extremists never see conditions as they exist, especially if it is a problem concerned with vice," he said. The biased attitude of the reformers "is only the logical outcome of their gross ignorance of the true conditions."[4]

Vollmer's long career in policing had its beginnings in the antivice crusades of the early years of this century, and his strong revulsion against political interference in policing was rooted in his memory of the wholesale corruption that surrounded vice law enforcement. In this reaction, Vollmer was one of many Americans whose concern for police reform dated from the excesses of those days.

The antivice crusaders from the period between 1905 to 1915 often attacked the police directly for lax law enforcement. Haller wrote that "perhaps the most important impact of the campaign against vice was the impetus it gave to the *gradual* professionalization of American urban police." After this time, "while scandals would periodically be uncovered, the police would seldom be the main object of the reform. . . ."[5]

Vice law enforcement was obviously the greatest threat that existed in those days to Vollmer's vision of a professional police service. It led to his most serious problems in Los Angeles and scarred the policing of city after city that he surveyed through the years. Unenforceable laws opened up opportunities for dishonesty on all levels.

In his own city, Vollmer's success in meeting the issue was considerably aided by the community support he received. Prohibition laws were effectively enforced in Berkeley, and there were accounts

[4] *The Police and Modern Society* (Montclair, N.J.: Patterson Smith, 1971, reprinted from 1936 ed.), pp. 81-82.

[5] Mark Haller, "Theories of Criminal Violence and Their Impact on the Criminal Justice System," in *Crimes of Violence*, National Commission on the Causes and Prevention of Violence, vol. 13 (Washington, D.C.: U.S. Government Printing Office, 1969), p. 1332, emphasis in original.

that gambling and prostitution were also largely absent. Opportunities for vice in nearby San Francisco and Oakland doubtless helped, and Vollmer was able to maintain higher standards of honesty within his department than a chief in a large city could have hoped for.

Vollmer believed that even if a community supported loose enforcement of vice laws, a chief could not afford politically to lower standards in this area. When someone queried him about department policy in another matter—children playing in the streets—he replied that the "police will not be looking for violations of this character, but when they are called to the attention of this department we cannot refuse to act."[6] All police departments exercise this sort of discretion in cases where violations are tolerated by the community. But such a policy was impossible, in his view, where liquor violations, prostitution, and gambling were concerned.

There were repeated cases of police chiefs losing their jobs over public criticism of illegal operations that the department ignored, even if the police limited the illegal activity through informal regulation. In an exchange of letters with a citizen about a chief in Colorado Springs who had followed the lead of an "easy-going administration," Vollmer acknowledged that police policies were often determined in these areas by the commissioners; but he asserted that he "can never agree with the chief who permits himself to be so used."[7]

Walter Petersen of the Oakland department, who put Vollmer in contact with Los Angeles gamblers in 1923, delivered a paper on this issue before the 1916 meeting of the International Association of Chiefs of Police. He titled it "The Chief of Police: The Goat for the Sins of Society." "It is a popular fiction that majorities rule our cities, but as a matter of fact the majorities of our cities are so much concerned with making money and living, that they, the majority, permit the minority to rule. ..." His view of the moral reformer was similar to that of Vollmer: The police chief "should not be concerned if a crowd of hysterical women denounce him or unsexed men abuse him."[8]

At the time, Chief Petersen was under attack by reform groups in Oakland for the police tolerance to gambling that eventually led

[6] Letter dated Jan. 27, 1925, to City Manager John Edy, Vollmer Collection, Bancroft Library, University of California, Berkeley.
[7] Letter dated June 26, 1916, to Mr. D. F. Carpenter, Vollmer Collection.
[8] Published in the *Proceedings of the I.A.C.P.*, 1916.

to his ouster. Leaders of these groups circulated a letter attacking Petersen during this meeting and effectively destroyed his chances to win his campaign that year to become president of the association.

Vollmer's own opinions about vice problems were realistic and nonpunitive. Of prostitution he wrote: "Statistics show that arrest for prostitution is ineffective in eliminating this vice." He favored public health involvement to control venereal disease and recommended leaving the "moral aspects" to "parents, clergy, and the public educators."[9] One colleague speculated that Vollmer's approval of the idea of "red light districts" stemmed from his roots in New Orleans, where it was an established tradition.[10]

Writing about the large-scale gambling raids that characterized the era and which he himself conducted in Berkeley and Los Angeles, Vollmer complained: "Thus goaded to action by charges brought by pulpit and press, the police are made the unwilling agents through whom futile injustices are inflicted upon thousands of innocent people." He considered this function such a threat to the integrity of the police that he suggested its total removal from the regular police force.

In this area, enforcement of the laws—even on a professional basis—destroyed the ability of the policeman to maintain credibility with the public. It was a fatal distraction from the policeman's primary job, "the protection of society from professional criminals."[11]

His objections to Prohibition were similar. Writing shortly after the law's repeal, he approved of maintaining some regulation over the liquor industry to prevent the widespread abuses that led to the antisaloon movement, but because of the potential for corruption, he recommended that any enforcement should be assigned to a separate agency. "Repression in any form should by all means be taken from the police, who are charged with the responsibility of preventing crime, and assigned to a new agency."[12]

Prohibition laws had been enforced lethargically through much of the 1920s, and when Hoover instituted a drive for honest and efficient enforcement after 1928, the damage was probably too great

---

[9] *The Police and Modern Society, op. cit.*, pp. 90-92.
[10] Unpublished interview with Spencer D. Parratt, 1973.
[11] *The Police and Modern Society, op. cit.*, pp. 95-100.
[12] *Ibid.*, p. 108.

to be undone. Radical enforcement at an early stage would probably have led either to success or rapid repeal.[13]

Drug abuse is the only one of these issues that continues to elicit as much emotionalism now as during earlier decades. Vollmer's suggestions in this area resemble the nonpunitive position that is taken by modern reformers. "In the popular notion the number of criminals that use drugs is greatly exaggerated," he asserted. The total number of crimes may be large, but they are "numerous minor crimes committed by a few drug users. . . . Major crimes committed by 'drug-soaked fiends' are comparatively rare." He considered the problem one for medical treatment and education. "The eradication of drug addiction by short jail sentences has proved a futile effort." Drug dispensaries should be established by the government, thus removing the profit motive and the "drug peddlar."[14]

In summary, Vollmer felt that enforcement of vice laws created disastrous problems within a police agency. It opened the way for wholesale corruption of policemen; it led to "revolving-door" tenures for police executives; it consumed an inordinate amount of police time and manpower; and it jeopardized the relationship of respect and cooperation between the policeman and the citizen.

Vollmer perceived this need for public credibility most clearly where vice laws were concerned. He dreamed of a legal system that would leave the police free to pursue their "real" work, the suppression of serious crime. His hostility toward vice law enforcement provided a major impetus for his concept of professional policing, in which the policeman would be unfettered by the entanglements of political corruption and organized crime and above the factionalism produced by diverse moral codes.

MIDDLE-CLASS POLICEMEN

In addition to their antipathy toward vice and corruption, reformers shared a desire to make the policeman "more like us," to give him education and more subtle techniques than the third degree he had relied on in the past; to remove him from the lower class or immigrant culture of nineteenth century policing and ensure that

[13] Andrew Sinclair, *Prohibition: The Era of Excess* (Boston: Little, Brown, 1962), pp. 212-214.

[14] *The Police and Modern Society, op. cit.*, pp. 109-110.

his values were closer to those of the middle class. This meant removing him from the control of the "machines," of the corrupt officials who controlled many city governments. The values and skills of policing should transcend the comings and goings of various municipal administrations.

It was a hospitable climate for professionalism. Two of Vollmer's associates were involved in an effort to rate the effectiveness of police departments during the mid-1930s that indirectly cast some light upon the specifics of the public attitude at that time. Arthur Bellman, a lawyer and student of police administration in Berkeley, published a rating scale for the evaluation of police departments that was based entirely on internal criteria.[15] It was a cumbersome, multicategory list of procedures and equipment that a modern department should have. Bellman explicitly denied the right of citizens to participate in the evaluation of their police. "It is the responsibility of police bodies to do the job entrusted to them to the best of their ability, regardless of public attitude."[16] Detachment from partisan politics led to detachment from citizen involvement as well; only the professional had both the knowledge to judge police performance and the commitment to rise above competing claims upon police services.

The Bellman scale was challenged by Spencer Parratt, the political scientist who had worked with Vollmer since the Los Angeles survey and was working on issues in public administration at Syracuse University. He criticized the scale for its ambiguity and failure to provide a basis for the weightings of various items. How could the "quality" of a police department be measured?[17]

With Vollmer's encouragement, Parratt continued his own research in this area, which had the goal of determining the characteristics that a cross-section of citizens wanted their police to have. He was attempting to devise an instrument that could serve as a basis for a scale to measure police effectiveness. His survey research, published in 1938, provided a good barometer of public attitudes toward police practices.[18]

Parratt found that the public wanted a police force that was

[15] "A Police Service Rating Scale," *Journal of Criminal Law and Criminology,* 26 (1935).

[16] *Ibid.,* p. 75.

[17] "A Critique of the Bellman Police Service Rating Scale," *ibid.,* 27 (1937).

[18] "A Scale to Measure Effectiveness of Police Functioning," *ibid.,* 28 (1938).

disciplined, effective, well equipped, and nonpolitical. Policemen should treat the public with respect; they should be neat and military in their appearance; they should have no contaminating contacts with politics, should possess at least average intelligence, and should take "professional interest" in their work. Little concern was expressed for the rights of minority groups as such. Harsher treatment was endorsed for "ex-convicts, Negroes, aliens, radicals, and gangsters"; "due process" did not emerge as a positive value, despite occasional responses to the contrary.

Above all, there was almost no interest in citizen participation in the policy making process. Respondents seemed to accept or even favor the notion of an expert police department that would fight crime and would be isolated from corrupting political influences. They wanted the police to be more decorous in conduct and appearance and more efficient in combating crime; they seemed more interested in *civility* than in civil rights or civil liberties. They were not concerned with police conduct in areas that did not affect them directly and were uninterested in the larger issue of the just use of police power against all citizens.

In devising his scale for use by the "expert police administrator," Parratt was hoping to ally him with citizen opinion in forming policies for his department. He believed that an objective measure of police functioning would prevent partisan political interests from obscuring the nature of police policies. "There can be no mumbo-jumbo of the politician whenever more explicit devices can be utilized."[19] The expertise of the administrator would be combined with an enlightened understanding of public opinion, an alliance that would effectively bypass the political process.

POLICING ABOVE THE FRAY

The most basic impulse behind the shaping of professional policing was the desire to remove the police from the partisan battleground in order to prevent them from being used as corrupt and passive pawns in the power struggles within the cities. The neutrality that the professional ideology imparted was sufficient to shift attention from the police to other institutions. Moral reformers, although convinced that policing was in need of reform, were less

[19] *Ibid.*, 756.

likely to place it in the camp of the "forces of evil" with which they warred. As Haller has pointed out, "the police joined in the [deterrent] tradition, and helped to divert attention upon the courts and parole boards as the primary factors chiefly responsible for undermining effective law enforcement."[20] Moral reformers in the psychological and sociological traditions focused their attention upon issues of poor schools, weak family structure, inadequate medical care, and crude forms of economic exploitation in the world of work.

Of more lasting influence in the drive for municipal change were the civic reformers who organized in protest against violence and rising property crime and, accordingly, against the governmental institutions that were failing to protect their middle-class constituency. Vollmer's professionalism was fully attuned to these demands in promising to fight crime aggressively and to remain free of the disreputable machinery of partisan politics. Vollmer was himself a civic reformer in his reaction against the traditional corruption of municipal government and his skepticism of the goals of moral reformers.

These were trends that affected policing from the outside. They coincided with a rise in occupational consciousness within policing that brought pressure for improved working conditions. When unionism was ruled out as a possibility, professionalism became the most promising alternative. The characteristics of the professional image were in accord with citizen expectations. More recent concern that has arisen over issues of citizen participation and cultural diversity within policing seemed remote at a time when diversity was considered a threat to impartial policing and citizen participation meant the co-opting of police power for the furtherance of special goals.

Above all, the earlier period was marked by a fear of lawlessness that seemed to have eroded the faith of middle-class citizens in the functioning of local government. The writings of moral and civic reformers, of police scholars like Fosdick and Vollmer, reflected this conviction that the due process of the political machinery was not to be trusted.

Professionalism brought insularity into policing when it tried to protect it from corruption and from manipulation by diverse moral codes. Although most police departments only partly reflect the

[20] "Theories of Criminal Violence," op. cit., p. 1332.

idealized model that Vollmer constructed, professionalism provides them with an ideology that encourages them to function independent of local social conflict and with only formal direction from elected government.

7 IMPLICATIONS AND ALTERNATIVES

> Police is the second general division of jurisprudence. . . .
> [N]ow it only means the regulation of the inferior parts of
> government, viz: cleanliness, security, and cheapness or
> plenty. The two former, to wit, the proper method of carrying
> dirt from the streets and the execution of justice, so far as
> it regards regulations for preventing crimes or the method
> of keeping a city guard, though useful, are too mean to be
> considered in a general discourse of this kind. An observation
> or two . . . is all that is necessary.
>
> Adam Smith, *Lectures on Justice, Police,*
> *Revenue, and Arms* (1763)

PROFESSIONALISM IN A CRIMINAL JUSTICE CONTEXT

For hopeful practitioners in criminal justice, the occupations of
policing, probation, and parole have come to be regarded as "emerging
professions."[1] Even those who are critical of contemporary police
practices tend to view professionalization as the best way to correct
the inefficiencies and unresponsiveness of big city departments.

In the process, professionalism has become a catchall concept
that is used to justify a wide variety of techniques and budget
expenditures. According to the 1967 President's Commission on Law
Enforcement and the Administration of Justice, "practically any
effort that is aimed at improving law enforcement" invokes the
sanction of "professionalization." The commission cites "improved
training, the application of the computer to police work, the adoption
of a code of ethics, and increased salaries" as examples.[2] To these

[1] L. C. Loughrey and H. C. Friese, Jr., "Criminal Justice Guidelines for
Educators and Practitioners," *The Police Chief*, 34, no. 8 (1967): 37.

[2] President's Commission on Law Enforcement and the Administration
of Justice, *Task Force Report: The Police* (Washington, D.C.: U.S. Government Printing Office, 1967), pp. 20-21.

may be added the pervading emphasis on crime control "by those who would 'professionalize' police work by focusing it more fully on crime control, transferring other functions to other municipal agencies."[3]

Criticism of police professionalism falls into two categories. The first has reference to police function by raising the question of whether or not the tasks that policemen perform are truly amenable to professionalization. "Certainly, there is much that police do today that would not, under any definition, be viewed as constituting professional work," wrote the commission, offering as an example the direction of traffic at a street intersection. "In sharp contrast, however, the beat patrolman assigned to police a congested, high crime area is called upon to make highly sophisticated judgments having a major impact upon the lives of the individuals involved."[4]

The second category of criticism has reference to the effect that the professional ideology has upon the attitude or stance of the police agency. Technological and managerial reforms make police work "less personal, more withdrawn from parts of the community, and less sensitive to the variety of human situations."[5] James Q. Wilson saw professionalism as "probably impossible" unless "honesty, efficiency, impartiality, and the impersonal application of general rules" are highly valued in the city where it is attempted. Further, professional policing "in principle at least, devalues citizen opinion *as manifested in personal relations*; professionalism, in this sense, means *impersonalization*."[6]

If we attempt to understand police professionalism by relating it to traditional professions like medicine and the law, the differences become quickly apparent. Vollmer was fond of saying that policing should be upgraded into a "science" on the level of the more venerable professions, but the analogy is too misleading to be of real assistance in police reform.

What elements are necessary in an occupation that aspires to professional status? An idealized definition follows.

[3] Jameson W. Doig, "Police Problems, Proposals, and Strategies for Change," *Public Administration Review,* 28 (1968): 395.

[4] *Op. cit.,* p. 21.

[5] David J. Bordua and Edward W. Haurek, "The Police Budget's Lot," *American Behavioral Scientist,* 13 (1970): 673.

[6] James Q. Wilson, "Police Morale, Reform, and Citizen Respect: The Chicago Case," in *The Police: Six Sociological Essays,* ed. David J. Bordua (New York: John Wiley, 1967), pp. 139, 160, emphasis in original.

A profession is a vocation whose practice is founded upon an understanding of the theoretical structure of some department of learning or science, and upon the abilities accompanying such understanding. This understanding and these abilities are applied to the vital practical affairs of man. The practices of the profession are modified by knowledge of a generalized nature and by the accumulated wisdom and experience of mankind, which serve to correct the errors of specialism. The profession, serving the vital needs of man, considers its first ethical imperative to be altruistic service to the client.[7]

This definition—more a religious creed than a job description—is obviously inapplicable to the great majority of occupations currently seeking professional status and benefits, although it may serve as an ultimate goal for idealists within any occupation.

Mosher, writing about public service occupations in general, formulated a more liberal and useful definition of professionalism by which we may judge the claims of criminal justice workers: The professional must have a reasonably clearcut occupational field; he should be required to hold at least a bachelor's degree; and the occupation should offer a lifetime career.[8] This practical schema omits the altruistic and esoteric elements that are associated with traditional professionalism. It is an accurate description of the foundation upon which many public service occupations—in criminal justice, social services, health planning and recreation—seek to build professional status for themselves.

Yet even by these standards, police work falls far short of meeting the criteria that fields like social work and probation have achieved in many localities. There are more policemen and policewomen with bachelor's degrees every year, but they still comprise a small minority of all police officers. Difficulty is also encountered in referring to policing as a "clearcut occupational field." Patrol work is the heart of policing, the most constant and abiding function and that which involves the greatest manpower. Specialized crime solving work usually engages only a minority of investigators or criminalists within the department. The more specialized aspects of traffic engineering may be entirely separated from the department itself. Finally, the

[7] Morris L. Cogan, "The Problem of Defining a Profession," *Annals of the American Academy*, 297 (1955): 107.

[8] Frederick C. Mosher, *Democracy and the Public Service* (New York: Oxford University Press, 1968), p. 106.

idea of the police officer as a skilled social worker or crime preventer is irrelevant to the actual work of the police in most cities. Although individual officers may be perceptive and generous in dealing with people's problems, their skills in performing this work stem from character and attitude, not from higher education.

Taken together, these elements do not comprise enough of a clearcut occupational field to support an educational curriculum of professional quality. A four-year program of higher education will impart to future policemen about what it imparts to other students, that is, perhaps a wider view of the world and a general heightening of skills needed to function successfully in any occupation.

The current drive for police professionalism is part of a wider movement among public service occupations to increase internal influence over policy making and to minimize outside influence over the evaluation and nature of the work performed. One writer has characterized aspects of the new professionalism as "galloping specialization, university-based credentialism, continuing education, ... prolonged adolescence, and serial careerism."[9] In the transition from the old to the new professionalism, a change has been made "from savant to specialized expert ... and from independent gentleman to a new form of hired help."[10]

The lack of independent power of these new professional groups is obvious. Indeed, the assertion of professional competence by workers within policing and other criminal justice occupations may be interpreted as a reaction against their dependence upon the bureaucratic structures that employ them—as a high form of trade unionism.

There are also political reasons for the acceptance of professionalism by elected officials. Police policies are a volatile realm of city government, and when a department claims to be operating from a professional stance, it provides a protective distance for officials who, under the old system, would have been held directly responsible for police actions. The public is also willing to allow difficult policies to be determined behind a shield of professional expertise, granting to the specialist authority over areas of public life that seem too complicated for citizen control. A professionalized agency invariably receives more support and prestige than the bureaucratic one it may have supplanted because bureaucracy is associated in the public mind

[9] Bertram M. Gross, "Planning in an Era of Social Revolution," *Public Administration Review*, 31 (1971): 277.

[10] *Ibid.*, quoting Gilb.

with insensitivity and with an excessive zeal for procedure, and it cannot claim that its actions are above lay judgment.

Although it is useful to consider police professionalism as part of the larger drive for professional status by many occupations, there are special elements in policing that make professionalism a more dangerous choice than in other fields. Most prominent of these elements is the inherently elitist nature of police work. The professional's claim to expertise, to the right to define his job and the techniques he may use, to "know better" than the uninitiated removes him from the political context of his work. When professionalism as an ideology is applied to police work, it reinforces the tendency of the police to exercise discretion in difficult areas away from public view. Police elitism has the additional characteristic that policemen feel their occupation to be held in low repute by the public; as an elite "pariah" class, in their view, policemen are moralistic and tend to become cynical when confronted with ambiguous directions.

Elitism also tends to suppress innovation unless it is introduced by those who are already fully socialized into police work. New ideas from outside sources are extremely suspect and are rarely adopted. Suggestions coming from the general public are regarded as too simplistic or uninformed. Since the alternatives already present within policing do not represent the total alternatives available, elitism becomes a handicap to innovation.

When contemporary citizens concern themselves with the characteristics of the policing in their city, they are only indirectly dealing with the professional model that Vollmer applied during his career. Under the direction of practitioners like O. W. Wilson and William Parker, professionalism evolved into a managerial model that minimized key elements of Vollmer's policing, such as crime prevention through positive community action and the view of the policeman as a committed public servant. Another way to describe this shift is to point out that Vollmer emphasized the professional police officer; later applications were more concerned with the professional agency. Professionalism became less of an individual characteristic and more the sum of many components within a department.

Skolnick has described the managerial approach as one that emphasizes "rationality, efficiency, and universalism." The professional is seen as a "bureaucrat, almost as a machine calculating alternative courses of action by a stated program of rules, and possessing the technical ability to carry out decisions irrespective of personal feelings."[11] Although elements of rationality, efficiency, and universalism were certainly important in Vollmer's concept of professionalism, they were subordinate to his view of the police officer as a benevolent and skilled crime fighter.

Some Positive Aspects of the Professional Model

Criticism of the direction of police reform does not prevent the recognition that many of the fruits of that reform were desirable at the time they emerged and that they continue to provide legitimate answers to ongoing police problems. On the technical side, the most obvious of these benefits of reform is the professional approach to traffic regulation, a systemic concern that is amenable to utilitarian values. It favors an impersonal approach that maximizes system benefits and measures the individual policeman's efforts against the standard of efficiency. The public has come to take for granted the existence of a body of expertise in traffic regulation and engineering that was unknown in the earlier years of this century, and it was policemen in the professional tradition who saw the need for rationality in traffic regulation and developed the skills to supply it. It is reasonable to suggest that the traffic function, which consumes an increasing part of the resources of many police departments, be assigned to a separate municipal agency that is organized primarily around this task.

The public would also not give up technological competence and efficiency in the investigation of serious crime. The modern crime investigator, having access to a scientific crime laboratory, has a secure position in future policing. It is a genuine specialty requiring specialized study and drawing upon a body of expertise that includes sophisticated contributions from medicine and the physical and biological sciences.

Most police departments have access to these facilities through their state police or through the Federal Bureau of Investigation. There is little need for a municipal department to retain line personnel who are skilled in scientific analysis or forensic medicine or to insist that line officers develop these skills. The existence of this definable specialty should not affect the personnel standards and functional organization of an entire department. Criticisms of police profes-

[11] Jerome H. Skolnick, *Justice Without Trial* (New York: John Wiley, 1967), p. 236.

sionalism need not imply a return to the imprecise and uninformed techniques of crime solving of the last century. The technical skills that officers within a local department should retain—in photography and evidence collection, for instance—do not require a high degree of advanced training and need not be used as a standard for recruitment.

The other elements that we would preserve from Vollmer's model of police professionalism are less easy to define. He and some of his contemporaries introduced an ethic of honesty and dedication to counter the cynical view of police service that had been prevalent in its earlier days. Policing was demoralized when Vollmer entered it, and he was part of a movement that imparted some dignity and high purpose into police work. Although tensions remain high between policemen and some segments of the public—and police morale constantly reflects these tensions—the occupation is not considered as disreputable as most citizens of the last century viewed it.

In sum, professionalism has upgraded the occupation of policing in many ways. It has served as a vehicle for many specific reforms or innovations that would have met an indifferent reception in the old style departments where efficiency was a low priority and where little concern was given to the welfare of the individual patrolman. The more basic problems within the professional model emerged when it ceased being an *unarticulated approach* for reform and became a *rigid ideology.*[12]

DETACHMENT VERSUS PARTICIPATION

If the crime fighting priority may be singled out as professionalism's dominant trait, its two most important corollaries are *detachment from the community* and *centralization of authority and organization.* The first of these is the direct result of the forces discussed in the previous chapter, whereby policemen reacted in defense against conflicting pressures upon them by detaching themselves from both politicians and the public. This avenue of reform was a key aspect of the Vollmer model and was also endorsed by the leading police scholars of the first half of the century.

The issue of detachment contains within it the question of civilian

[12] See Robert H. Wiebe, *The Search for Order: 1877-1920* (New York: Hill & Wang, 1967), pp. 222-223.

control of police actions. Political decision making at the local level is the only procedure available to the American citizen for the visible or self-evident control of his local police. Unlike other models, the American police have historically been closely associated with political decision making, both formal and informal, rather than with rule by law. Accountability of the police must be political because the unclear nature of their enforcement duties makes legal accountability difficult.

Westley wrote of this defensive insularity of the police in connection with the "increasing reliance on violence and secrecy by the police" that follows sharp criticism.

> Professionalization, which has been the major goal of modern police administrators during the past two decades, has the effect of insulating the police from public pressures. . . . Yet we must be wary since insulation from political influence without other methods of integration, such as a positive relationship to the community, can mean insulation from all of us, and if the goals of the police should vary from those of the citizens, it can become a very serious problem.[13]

When detachment is combined with an emphasis on technical expertise, the citizen becomes not only an amateur but incompetent as well. He is prevented from participating in police policy making on the double grounds that participation would be "illegitimate interference" and would be based merely on ignorance.

Even many observers who call for more citizen participation in policing do not challenge the fundamental structural detachment of the police organization. Into this category fall the "citizen education" and other liaison committees that have been formed from time to time to provide an input from the community into policing. Parratt's view is a good example of this response to the problem of detachment.[14] He believed in an alliance between police administrators and citizen opinion, presumably through such technical devices as his public opinion survey. He did not challenge the right of the police administrator to be a detached expert but merely attempted to develop a method for channeling citizen views to him.

The alternative to detachment is a system of citizen participation

[13] William A. Westley, *Violence and the Police: A Sociological Study of Law, Custom, and Morality* (Cambridge, Mass.: The MIT Press, 1970), pp. xv-xvi.

that includes both formally structured civilian control over police policies and informal control through the decentralization of policing into community-based units. Existing official mechanisms for reviewing police decisions and determining police policy have proved inadequate in reflecting the attitudes of citizens toward their police department. In many cities, officials can only manipulate police policy by hiring and firing police leaders, who must be drawn either from within the department or from similarly professionalized departments. Routine decision making within the department is relatively inaccessible.

Participation should also work in two directions: from the citizen to the police and from the policeman to the political processes. The public is rightly apprehensive of political involvement by policemen when the police department itself remains detached and autonomous. But this is a denial of the citizenship rights of policemen as individuals and as an organization; it is only natural to expect that a policeman should want a voice in the processes that affect him. When routine citizen control of policing is established, objections to political activities by policemen will lose their rationale. A department that has an open recruitment policy and consciously maintains representation from all segments of the community is unlikely to become so entrenched in a single ideology as to endanger the ability of others to participate. Policemen are already involved in issues of their own working conditions through various forms of police unionism, which is no longer considered a threat but a reality.[15]

CENTRALIZATION VERSUS HOME RULE

Home rule or, on a smaller level, "community control," is another traditional American value that coexists uneasily with the ideology of professional policing. Although large-scale centralization of police authority has never taken root in the United States, professionalism favors many procedures and principles which accomplish similar results. Centralization of records is the most pervasive example; less tangible is the tendency for local police organizations to use common ideological interpretations in confronting the problems of their particular communities.

[14] See our discussion on pp. 104-105.

[15] See M. W. Aussieker, Jr., *Police Collective Bargaining* (Chicago: Public Personnel Association, 1969).

In 1909 the police scholar Fuld observed: "Among a free people most agencies of the government are decentralized, decentralization being a technical term for local home rule. We are, therefore, not at all surprised to find that the English police system was originally decentralized."[16] Decentralization or home rule is a tenet of democracy that does not necessarily produce efficiency in government, however, and often works against it. Efficiency became an early goal of police professionalism and, buttressed by public fears of crime, was rarely questioned. Vollmer was entirely right in pointing out that local jurisdictional boundaries interfered with the efforts of police administrators to fight crime and maintain the public order.

The positive values of home rule are often overlooked when efficiency becomes the overriding measure. Local autonomy has been one way for a community to ensure that its department was responsive to local priorities rather than to centralized state or national goals. Except in areas like traffic (and even in this case there are considerable local variations), police professionalism has been unable to change the fact that routine police tasks remain overwhelmingly local in their orientation.

This misperception of goals that is encouraged by police professionalism produces its own kinds of inefficiency. Many departments, by adhering to the professional ideology, expend their resources upon goals that are minimally related to the work they are called upon to do. In one municipality in southern Alameda County, California, the police department used federal money to train and equip a "Special Occurrences" or riot squad, although the city had never had a civil disturbance and had no indication that one was expected. The squad was used several times in a neighboring city where disturbances did occur. The citizens of the home community, however, never received any direct benefit from this diversion of men and resources. In fact, the chief indicated in an interview that the highest priority for his own city was traffic control.

The local orientation of most police tasks is the first casualty of centralization in policing. A further casualty is the principle of home rule itself, which is intrinsically related to the problem of detachment. A centralized police department is by necessity detached; mechanisms for connecting it to smaller community units will always

[16] Leonhard F. Fuld, *Police Administration: A Critical Study of Police Organizations in the United States and Abroad* (Montclair, N.J.: Patterson Smith, 1971, reprinted from 1909 ed.), pp. 17-18.

be artificial and a posteriori, having little impact upon the overall organization of the department or the actions of its personnel.

The problem of police centralization on this level exists primarily within single jurisdictions like large, heterogeneous cities, where neighborhoods or ethnic communities demand increased power over policing in their areas. The first goal in this direction is local minority recruitment, which is only a technical device to ensure increased power through physical representation. The second goal is a structural decentralization of the police department itself, in which local communities will have control over routine police policy but can avail themselves of centralized facilities for a minimum of technical services.

The more subtle form of centralization is present in the adoption of the professional ideology by departments having widely varying priorities. Riot squads in homogeneous middle-class suburbs is one example; police supervision of school crossing guards in Harlem is another. Overall, the professional ideology tends to shape a department's priorities irrespective of local conditions and to encourage recruitment and training practices that are unrepresentative as well as inefficient.

The more formal centralization of policing that Vollmer advocated has not occurred for several reasons, one of the strongest being the opposition over the years of organized labor to a structure that could be used against efforts to organize and strike. But ideological centralization has succeeded in creating an atmosphere wherein decisions are based on professional police theory and values rather than the actual goal of a particular policy.

Misner documented this situation in his study of policing at the 1964 Republican National Convention in San Francisco.[17] Nonviolent but widely publicized demonstrations occurred, during which the police maintained a low profile. Area policemen later expressed the opinion that their efforts at the convention had been a failure, even though the press and political leaders on all levels had praised them at the time for using restrained tactics that contributed to keeping the peace at the convention.

[17] Gordon E. Misner, *Police Minority Group Relations at the 1964 Republican National Convention* (Doctoral dissertation, University of California, Berkeley, 1967).

Professional Approaches to Policy Making

By asserting their professionalism, modern police administrators claim the right to formulate policy at a considerable distance from the political process. In those cities where policing is further removed from *vox populi* through the interposition of a professional city manager, these important policy areas become remote from citizen intervention.

The managerial approach to policing, cited above, becomes the accepted mode for problem solving. The old style of policy making was described by the President's 1967 commission as "unarticulated improvisation," to which is opposed the more modern approach that "anticipates social problems and adapts to meet them before a crisis situation arises."[18]

There are doubtless other, more neutral areas in which the tools of administration and policy analysis can make a genuine contribution. Policing, however, is inextricably enmeshed in a "political culture," as James Q. Wilson characterized it,[19] and those aspects of urban life that most urgently confront police administrators are least accessible to solution through their administrative skills.

Another view of the realities of policy formation was given by a writer in discussing the inexactitude of national foreign policy: "Anyone who has had anything to do with any government knows what a conventional fiction it is to speak of governments making policy decisions as though this were a detached and rational process." Instead, "decisions tend to build up like coral reefs from the accretion of small unobserved deposits."[20]

Important political questions are almost by definition intractable to administrative solutions, and the issues of group conflict and social coercion that surround police policy making are far beyond constructive manipulation by the skills of professional policing. As new interest groups and issues emerge in the community, they are more likely to be recognized and accommodated through an approach that includes the conscious use of the kind of "improvisation" that a

[18] *Op. cit.*, p. 18.
[19] *Varieties of Police Behavior* (Cambridge, Mass.: Harvard University Press, 1968), p. 233.
[20] M. Shulman, "Relations with the Soviet Union," in K. Gordon, ed., *Agenda for the Nation* (Garden City, N.Y.: Doubleday & Co., 1968), p. 392.

politically responsive department will develop. When the political nature of policing is denied, the subsequent reliance on administrative expertise tends merely to isolate symptoms of problems, attempting to resolve them without a view of the larger pattern.

The black revolution of the 1960s, for example, grew out of a disproportion in the political sensitivity of the body politic as a whole. Improvement in police sensitivity through sophisticated policy making may avoid certain crises, but only at a long-range cost that should be apparent to the public that is responsible for real solutions. Too often, police efforts to accommodate the demands of minority groups have been mere "public relations," however sincere may have been their motivation. The ideology of professionalism automatically excludes a whole range of variances in police organization that would be more substantive; decentralization of authority, an open attack upon overt and institutional racism within the department, and an adjustment of policing styles in minority neighborhoods are examples. There is a greater neutrality or "professionalism" in these efforts than in the use of professional ideology to mask a department's imposition of majority standards and fears upon a particular community.

LOWERING THE STAKES

What would be a more realistic orientation to replace that of the professional crime fighter, detached from the community and operating from an ideological perspective? We would suggest a *leveling of functions* that would place all the policeman's services on approximately the same scale; he could as rightly be judged for his efforts in referring drunks to detoxification centers as for apprehending a burglar. The miscellaneous, nonrational nature of public demands upon policing is an indisputable fact. Why not organize policing around this reality and at the same time keep it based in local priorities? Those specialized functions that a modern police department requires—sophisticated traffic engineering or crime analysis—can be supplied by centralized agencies or by personnel who enter the department laterally.

An accompanying change would be a *decrease in the importance of the overall police function*. Professionalism, as seen through the words of Vollmer and most of his successors, makes high promises about the ability of the police to control crime and maintain social order if only the public will grant the mandate and supply the necessary funds and autonomy. Part of the ideology of professionalism is the existence of an expertise that can cope with many social problems or that can reduce levels of violent crime. These claims— often forwarded in the context of the drive for increased status and better working conditions for policemen—are obviously exaggerated, and professional policing bears some of the responsibility for public ire when crime rates are not contained.

The inherent contradiction in singling out the police as providers of social order is the historical fact that municipal police can only exist when a state of social order is already in effect; their existence *presupposes* the state they claim to provide. [21] During times of civil unrest or more visible political turmoil, when the fundamental political order is either held to principle, questioned, or challenged, Vollmer's ideology encourages the public to become angry and to turn upon the police for failing to maintain order instead of looking at the larger and more persistent problems within the society. It is at these times that, according to Westley's description, the police turn to "violence and secrecy."[22] They are defending themselves against demands that they cannot fulfill, and they interpret this failure as resulting from the hostility of the public.

When local conditions lead to a state of riot or civil disorder, as defined by government officials, the most effective organization to meet that state of disorder would be a centralized military body, either the army or the national guard. The military possesses entirely different strategies than the police for dealing with disturbances, and its presence is a clear indication to the whole community that a crisis of order exists. It is not being asked to deal with a situation in which it is itself a key factor, as the police are, even if only in a symbolic way. Being organized in a centralized, military fashion, soldiers will also not encounter the problems of individual discretion and accountability that policemen always face. Westley recommended that there should be a "decrease in the duties leading to violent

[21] See the discussion by T. S. Smith in "Notes on Democratic Control and Professionalism in Police Systems" (Working Paper No. 90, University of Chicago Center for Social Organization Studies, 1967).

[22] *Op. cit.*, p. xv.

[23] *Ibid.*, p. xviii.

confrontation with the public, for example, riot control." He favored the use of the national guard over the army because it is a "broad citizen group."[23]

The ultimate justification for the use of the military, however, is not tactical but political; disorders of this extent are an indication of a challenge to the state's authority. Whether one interprets that challenge as legitimate or illegitimate, it is deceptive to view it as a "police problem." When state suppression on that scale is required, it should be open and obvious, it should interfere with business and bus schedules, and it should become an unavoidable part of the total life of the community. Inability to contain such a situation should not be seen as a failure of local policing anymore than the police of Vollmer's day "failed" to enforce liquor and gambling laws.

Profound social conflicts can only be resolved when the groups involved have access to the democratic exchange process;[24] there is no other mechanism in the United States for problem solving. Vollmer's professional policing, by placing the maintenance of order above the rights of all groups to have such access, perpetuates the very situation that is used to justify its existence. Although the police are not an important institution in themselves, their position as the maintainers of this inequity makes it imperative that control of policing be dispersed.

The risks involved would be greatly reduced if the importance of the police function were lowered to its traditional level. Municipal policing has much more to do with mediation and service functions than with riot control. Should neighborhoods break into open and extensive conflict, the United States is well supplied with military organizations which would be available to institute truly professional, legalistic control for the duration of the emergency. The only real decision that a policeman has is the power to arrest. All the long-term, more serious penalties of the criminal justice system cannot be invoked without the cooperation of the courts.

Centralized police departments in large American cities have more in common with standing armies than with historical policing. Their size alone undermines the entire rationale of civilian police. It is futile to expect that any amount of tinkering with police functions

[24] For a discussion of some issues surrounding decentralized police models, see Gene E. Carte, "In Defense of Alternative Policing: A Reply to James Q. Wilson," *Criminal Law Bulletin*, 8, no. 3 (1972): 207-216.

or any quest for democratic policemen with law degrees could bring policing into line with the expectations of the community. The same impasse is evident in large city school systems, which are under attack from all sides for being entrenched, inefficient, and failing to educate children.

Police cannot be expected to be accountable to a broader level of citizen interests unless those citizens receive some power over the police department. Citizens cannot be expected to participate in government services if the structure of those services excludes all but the most legalistic of outside influences. Finally, policing cannot be made local if its important policy decisions are made at a higher level.

Appendix

CHRONOLOGY OF THE CAREER OF AUGUST VOLLMER

This chronology was probably compiled by Vollmer in the late 1940s. It is reproduced here without alteration.

1896 Assisted in organizing North Berkeley Volunteer Fire Department
1897 Awarded Berkeley Fireman medal
1898 Private G Battery U.S. Artillery (25 battles and engagements)
1900 Postal service
1905 Elected town marshal
1905 Installed complete bicycle patrol service
1906 Installed first red light recall system
1906 Installed first centralized police record system
1906 Installed first modus operandi system
1907 President California Association of Chiefs of Police
1907 Organized movement for reinstituting California State Bureau of Identification
1907 Member Berkeley Charity Organization
1907 President Berkeley S.P.C.A.
1908 Organized Berkeley Police School
1909 Appointed Chief of Police
1909 Vice President National Playground Association
1913 Organized motorcycle patrol service
1914 Organized first automobile patrol service
1914 Member of State Recreation Inquiry Commission
1914 Organized Berkeley Junior Police

1915   Conducted San Diego Police Department survey
1916   Reorganized Berkeley Police School (see *Journal of Criminal Law and Criminology*)
1916   Lecturer in criminology program during U.C. summer session
1916   Vice President California Mental Hygiene Society
1917   President Board of Managers of the State Bureau of Identification
1917   President State Institute of Criminal Law and Criminology
1918   Vice President American Institute of Criminal Law and Criminology
1918   Lecturer in U.S. Army school for intelligence officers
1919   Assisted in organizing Hawthorne School study of potential offenders
1919   With Doctor Jau Don Ball, Professor Brietweiser, and Doctor Virgil-Dickson began informal group meetings which became foundation for coordination council movement
1920   Assisted in organizing Alameda County Traffic Safety Commission
1921   Vice President International Association of Chiefs of Police
1921   Installed first* fingerprint system in this country
1921   Installed first handwriting classification system in this country
1921   Installed first instrument for the detection of deception by police
1921   Member of the Board of Directors Alameda County Health Center
1922   President International Association of Chiefs of Police
1923   Chief of Police in Los Angeles (on leave from Berkeley)
1923   Assisted in organizing L.A. Academy of Criminology
1923   Assisted in organizing L.A. Child Guidance Clinic
1923   Organized extension courses in police administration at U.S.C.
1923   Reorganized L.A. Police Department (see survey report)
1924   Lecturer at U.S.C. summer session (with President Von Kleinschmidt)
1924   Organized bond campaign to equip police department at cost of three million dollars
1924   Installed first aluminum street markers in America
1926   Distributed patrolmen according to beat formula developed with aid of members of Berkeley Police Department
1926   Assisted in organizing Berkeley Safety Traffic Commission
1926   Surveyed Havana Police Department
1926   Served as consultant for Detroit Police Department

*Single fingerprint system.

1927 Surveyed Chicago Police Department (see report of Illinois Crime Survey)

1927 Police consultant for National Crime Commission (see report)

1928 Kansas City, Missouri, police survey

1929 Police consultant for National Law Observance and Enforcement Commission

1929 Member U.S. Federation of Justice

1929 Professor of Police Administration at University of Chicago (two year leave of absence from Berkeley Police Department)

1929 Harmon Foundation Medal for contributions to social science

1929 Organized National Conference to Expedite Uniform Crime Reporting

1930 Assisted in organizing Chicago Regional Peace Officers Association

1930 Organized movement to create Illinois State Identification Bureau

1930 With Doctors Ralph Webster and Harry Hoffman formed Chicago Academy of Criminology

1930 Minneapolis police survey

1930 Gary police survey

1930 With students in my classes made a survey of all police departments within fifty miles of Chicago

1931 Professor of Police Administration at University of California

1931 Assisted in organizing Police School at San Jose State College

1931 Benjamin Ide Wheeler award

1932 Retired as Chief of Police

1932 Assisted in organizing course for peace officers at L.A. Junior College

1932 With Kidd, Adler, Schmidt, and others assisted in organizing criminology curricula at University of California

1932 Trip around the world studying police methods

1934 National Academy of Sciences Public Welfare Medal "in recognition of the application of scientific methods in police administration and crime prevention"

1934 Santa Barbara police survey

1934 Lecturer Police Administration at University of Hawaii summer session

1934 Member of the Board of Directors East Bay Regional Park District

1934 Portland police survey

1935 Piedmont police survey

1937 Retired from the University of California

1938 Member of Inter-State Crime Commission

1939   California Prison Association President
1943   Syracuse police survey
1944   Dallas police survey
1947   Portland police survey
1947   Member National Academy for Advancement of Criminology

Bibliography

This is an updated and revised version of a list of publications by Vollmer that he probably compiled in the 1940s.

1917   *San Diego Police Survey*, June 1, 1917.

"The School for Police as Planned at Berkeley," with Albert Schneider, *Journal of the American Institute of Criminal Law and Criminology*, 7 (1917): 877-898. Reports on the reorganization of the Berkeley Police School in 1916. Includes bibliography of materials used.

1918   "The Convicted Man—His Treatment While Before the Court," *The National Police Journal*, 2 (1918).

"Criminal Identification Bureau," *Journal of the American Institute of Criminal Law and Criminology*, 9 (1918): 322-325.

1919   "California State Bureau of Identification," *Journal of the American Institute of Criminal Law and Criminology*, 9 (1919): 479-482. Reports on the new bureau that Vollmer had been instrumental in establishing.

"The Policeman as a Social Worker," *The Policeman's News,* June 1919. Also printed in *The National Police Journal*, 4 (1919). An early statement of Vollmer's view of the policeman as a crime preventer.

"Revision of the Atcherley *Modus Operandi* System," *Journal of the American Institute of Criminal Law and Criminology*, 10 (1919):

229-274. Describes the system that Vollmer and Clarence D. Lee constructed for use in the Berkeley department.

1920 "Bureau of Criminal Records," *Journal of the American Institute of Criminal Law and Criminology,* 11 (1920): 171-180. Describes a model system for maintaining criminal records.

"Statement of Personal Beliefs," *Proceedings of the International Association of Chiefs of Police for 1920,* pp. 122-123. General statement of philosophy of policing.

1921 *"Modus Operandi," National Police Bulletin,* 1 (1920): 2-3.

"Practical Method for Selecting Policemen," *Journal of the American Institute of Criminal Law and Criminology,* 11 (1921): 571-581. Contains statement of Vollmer's strong belief in higher educational standards for policemen.

1922 "Aims and Ideals of the Police," *Journal of the American Institute of Criminal Law and Criminology,* 13 (1922): 251-257. A reprint of Vollmer's address as president of the I.A.C.P. for 1922.

"Narcotic Control Association of California," *Journal of the American Institute of Criminal Law and Criminology,* 13 (1922), 126-127.

1923 "Pre-Delinquency," *Journal of the American Institute of Criminal Law and Criminology,* 14 (1923): 279-283.

1924 *Los Angeles Police Department Survey,* 1923-1924, 241 pp. (I.G.S. Library, University of California, Berkeley.) Letter of submittal contains a statement of Vollmer's philosophy of policing.

1925 *Detroit Police Department Survey,* December 15, 1925.

1926 "Adequate Equipment and Efficient Personnel Essential for Success in Police Administration," *American City,* 38 (1926): 111-112.

Havana, Cuba, Police Survey. National Police Department General Report, August 31, 1926.

"The Policewoman and Pre-Delinquency," *The Police Journal,* 13 (1926): 32.

"Prevention and Detection of Crime as Viewed by a Police Officer," *Annals of the American Academy,* 125 (1926): 148-153.

"Treatment of Second Termers and Recidivists," *The Police Journal,* 13 (1926): 15-18. Calls for classification and rehabilitation for first offenders, harsher treatment for recidivists.

"We Can Prevent Juvenile Crime!" *Sunset,* 56 (1926): 32-33.

1927   "Criminal Statistics," *The Police Journal,* December 1927, pp. 10-15.

"The Recidivist from the Point of View of the Police Officer," *Journal of Delaware,* 2 (1927): 72-87.

"Statistics on Criminality," *Peace Officer,* 5 (1927): 7-8.

1928   "Coordinated Effort to Prevent Crime," *Journal of the American Institute of Criminal Law and Criminology,* 19 (1928): 196-210.

"Police Organization and Administration; with Discussions," *Public Management,* 10 (1928): 140-152.

"Vice and Traffic—Police Handicaps," *University of Southern California Law Review,* 1 (1928): 326-331.

1929   "Criminal Investigation," *Encyclopedia Britannica* (14th ed.), vol. 12, 558-559.

"The Police (in Chicago)," Chap. 8 in *The Illinois Crime Survey* (Chicago: Illinois Association for Criminal Justice, 1929). (Reprinted by Patterson Smith, Montclair, N.J., 1968).

"Science in Crime," *La Critique,* 4 (1929): 5.

Survey of the Metropolitan Police Department of Kansas City, Missouri (Kansas City Chamber of Commerce, March 1929), 165 pp.

1930   "Meet the Lady Cop," *Survey,* 63 (1930): 702-703.

"Police Progress in Practice and Principles," *International Association Identification Proceedings,* 16 (1930): 54-56.

"The Scientific Policeman," *The American Journal of Police Science,* 1 (1930): 8-12.

Survey of Police Department, Minneapolis, Minnesota (Minneapolis, 1930), 192 pp. (I.G.S. Library, University of California, Berkeley.)

1931   "Abstract of the Wickersham Police Report," *Journal of the American*

Institute of Criminal Law and Criminology, 22 (1931): 716-723.

"Case Against Capital Punishment in California." Special message to California State Legislature, April 1, 1931.

"Is the Third Degree Ever Necessary? Police Officials Give Their Views," *Western City,* 7 (1931): 27-28. Interviews with police chiefs from Portland, Tacoma, Pasadena, Los Angeles, and Berkeley.

"Outline of a Course in Police Organization and Administration," *American Journal of Police Science,* 2 (1931): 70-79. Includes bibliography.

Report on Police, National Commission on Law Observance and Enforcement, vol. 14 (Washington, D.C.: U.S. Government Printing Office, 1931). (Reprinted by Patterson Smith, Montclair, N.J., 1968.) Vollmer served as director of this volume and authored the chapters on the police executive.

1932   Introduction to *Lying and Its Detection: A Study of Deception and Deception Tests* by John A. Larson (Chicago: University of Chicago, 1932). (Reprinted by Patterson Smith, Montclair, N.J., 1969.)

"Police Administration," *Public Management,* 14 (1932): 21-22.

1933   "Police Beat," *Proceedings of the International Association of Chiefs of Police,* 40 (1933): 304-318.

"Police Methods Need Changes," *Oakland Tribune,* October 19, 1933.

"Police Progress in the Last Twenty-Five Years," *Proceedings of the International Association of Chiefs of Police,* 40 (1933): 319-327. Also printed in *Journal of the American Institute of Criminal Law and Criminology,* 24 (1933): 161-175.

Review of *Rural Crime Control* by Bruce Smith, *Columbia Law Review,* 33 (1933): 1471-1473.

1934   "Curriculum for Peace Officers, Los Angeles Junior College," *Journal of the American Institute of Criminal Law and Criminology,* 25 (1934): 138-140.

Development of the Curriculum in Police Organization and Administration. Typewritten ms. dated March 1934. (I.G.S. Library, University of California, Berkeley.)

Lectures in Police Administration (Honolulu: University of Hawaii, mimeograph publication, June 26, 1934). (I.G.S. Library, University of California, Berkeley.)

"Police Administration," *Municipal Yearbook 1934*, pp. 77-79.

Review of *Private Police* by J. P. Shalloo, *Journal of Criminal Law and Criminology*, 24 (1934): 982-983.

Survey of the Police Department, Santa Barbara, California. Typewritten ms. dated April 21, 1934. (I.G.S. Library, University of California, Berkeley.)

"Trends in Adult Guidance with the Misfits," *The Vocational Guidance Magazine*, 13 (1934): 50-51.

"Universal Registration," *Journal of the American Institute of Criminal Law and Criminology*, 25 (1934): 650-652.

"Vestigial Organs: The Diminishing Effectiveness of the Grand Jury and the Preliminary Hearing as Aids to Justice," *State Government*, 7 (1934): 91-94.

1935 *Crime and the State Police*, with Alfred E. Parker (Berkeley: University of California Press, 1935), 226 pp. Contains strong advocacy of state policing and centralization of police facilities.

"What Can Bar Associations Do to Improve Police Conditions?" *State Bar Journal of California*, 10 (1935): 44-46.

1936 *The Police and Modern Society* (Berkeley:University of California Press, 1936), 253 pp. (Reprinted, with an introduction by James Q. Wilson, by Patterson Smith, Montclair, N.J., 1971.) Vollmer's most complete analysis of police problems.

A Survey of the Piedmont Police Department. Typewritten ms. dated 1936. (I.G.S. Library, University of California, Berkeley.)

1940 Foreword to *Police Interrogation* by Lt. W. R. Kidd (New York: R. V. Basuino, 1940).

1942 "Criminal Investigation," Chap. 3 in *Elements of Police Science*, ed. Rollin Perkins (Brooklyn: The Foundation Press, 1942).

1944 *Report of Dallas Police Department Survey*, City of Dallas, Texas,

March-April 1944), 195 pp. (I.G.S. Library, University of California, Berkeley.)

1947 *Police Bureau Survey, City of Portland, Oregon* (Portland: University of Oregon, Bureau of Municipal Research and Service, 1947), 217 pp. (I.G.S. Library, University of California, Berkeley.)

1949 *The Criminal* (Brooklyn: The Foundation Press, 1949).

1950 Preface to *Daily Training Bulletin of the Los Angeles Police Department* by W. H. Parker, Chief of Police, Los Angeles Police Department, 1950. (Reprinted by Chas. C Thomas, Springfield, Ill., 1958.)

1951 *Police Organization and Administration*, with John P. Peper and Frank M. Boolsen (Sacramento: California State Dept. of Education, Bureau of Trade and Industrial Education, 1951), 217 pp. Written and prepared for use in connection with the California Peace Officer's Training Program.

1953 Foreword to *Public Relations and the Police* by G. Douglas Gourley (Springfield, Ill.: Chas. C Thomas, 1953).

       Introduction to *The Instrumental Detection of Deception* by Clarence D. Lee (Springfield, Ill.: Chas. C Thomas, 1953).

1954 Foreword to *Are You Guilty? An Introduction to the Administration of Criminal Justice in the United States* by William Dienstein (Springfield, Ill.: Chas. C Thomas, 1954).

       Foreword to *Police Work with Juveniles* by John P. Kenney and Dan G. Pursuit (Springfield, Ill.: Chas. C Thomas, 1954).

NOTE: Many of the above papers and other material not listed were presented over the years by Vollmer at annual meetings of the International Association of Chiefs of Police. Refer to the *Proceedings* during these years for complete information.

Index

Adler, Herman, 64, 80
American Federation of Labor, 38-39
American Institute of Criminal Law and Criminology, 28
Anticommunism, 72-73

Ball, Dr. Jau Don, 32; Hawthorne school study, 34-35; intelligence testing, 42
Bellman, Arthur, 104
Berkeley: before 1905, 18; support for innovation, 22; incorporation, 24; coordinating council, 35-36; fingerprinting campaign, 77; and success of professional policing, 97
Berkeley police, 41-53; bicycle patrol, 22; "college cops," 42-44; and other departments, 44; patrolman a generalist, 45; high internal standards, 46-48; job security, 47; Crime Prevention Division, 48; automobile allowances, 43, 50; and the press, 51-52; successful professional model, 97
Berkeley Police School, 26-28, 95
Berkeley Y.M.C.A., 72-73, 81
Boston police, 8, 9; 1919 strike, 37-40
Brereton, George, 43
Burgess, Ernest W., 64

California State Bureau of Criminal Identification and Investigation, 29-30
Capital punishment, 72
Centralized policing, 74ff., 87, 95, 116ff.
Charles C Thomas Publishing Co., 81
Chicago Crime Commission, 58
Chicago police, 11-12, 63

Civil service reform, 40-41; Vollmer's opposition to, 53
Coolidge, Gov. Calvin, 39
Crime and the State Police, 75
Crime, Crooks and Cops, 81
Crime prevention: Vollmer's views, 33-34; contrasted with O. W. Wilson, 79, 112-113; versus crime fighting, 88, 89, 97
Criminal, The, 32, 81-82
Criminality: pre-World War I theories, 31; Vollmer's interest in, 30ff.; *The Criminal*, 81-82

Dean, William F., 43
Dullea, Capt. Charles, 74

Education for policemen: Berkeley department, 26-28, 42-43; Vollmer's faith in, 69ff., 95-96
Edy, John N., 52
Elitism, ix, 112
European police models, 2, 8ff.

Federal Bureau of Investigation, 55-56, 113
Fosdick, Raymond: studies of policing, 2, 9; re police unions, 39; re civil service, 41; re Berkeley police, 53; re vice laws, 98
Fuld, Leonhard: re political corruption, 1; police study, 2; re foreign police models, 8-10; re centralization, 117
Function. *See* Police function

Gain, Charles, 80

135

Thompson, Hollis, 65
Thurstone, L., 64
Traffic control, 54, 89ff., 110, 113, 117

Universal registration, 76-77
University of California, 18; effect on
   Vollmer's ideas, 22; and early police
   education, 27-28; criminal justice pro-
   gram, 69; School of Criminology, 82
University of Chicago, 63-64

Vice law enforcement: in Berkeley, 47-48,
   100-101; in Alameda County, 48; in Los
   Angeles, 59, 61; and politics, 11, 98ff.
Vollmer, August: youth, 19-21; election as
   town marshal, 18-19; early innovations,
   22-23; police surveys, 29, 62-63; political
   views, 33; re police unionism, 39-40, 53;
   control over Berkeley department, 46-
   47; skill in public and press relations,
   29, 50ff.; I.A.C.P. presidency, 56-58; in

Los Angeles, 58ff.; at University of Chicago, 63-64; resignation as chief, 64-65;
   Wickersham Report, 66ff.; at University
   of California, 68ff.; re free speech and
   anticommunism, 72-73; and O. W. Wilson, 78-79; death, 82-83; re vice laws,
   100ff.

Warren, Earl, 48-49, 71
Westley, William A., 115, 121
Wickersham Report, 66ff.; re "third de-
   gree," 72; re centralized policing, 76
Wiebe, Robert, 40
Wilson, James Q., 7, 8, 86, 119
Wilson, O. W., 3; impact of Vollmer, 43-44;
   re Berkeley patrol function, 45; opposi-
   tion in Wichita, 52-53; contrasted with
   Vollmer, 78-79; dean at Berkeley, 82;
   managerial model, 112
Woods, Arthur, 33